Crafting Personal
SHRINES

Using Photos, Mementos & Treasures to Create Artful Displays

Crafting Personal
SHRINES

Carol Owen

LARK BOOKS
A Division of Sterling Publishing Co., Inc.
New York

DEDICATION

To my husband, Gwil, who has wanted me to do a book for many years—here it is, finally! He has been patient and supportive through 48 years of marriage. I couldn't have done it without his help.

EDITOR
Ronni Lundy

ART DIRECTOR
Susan McBride

COVER DESIGN
Barbara Zaretsky

ASSOCIATE ART DIRECTOR
Shannon Yokeley

ASSISTANT EDITOR
Nathalie Mornu

EDITORIAL ASSISTANCE
Delores Gosnell

EDITORIAL INTERN
Rebecca Guthrie

PHOTOGRAPHY
Keith Wright
keithwright.com

ILLUSTRATIONS
Orrin Lundgren

The Library of Congress has cataloged the hardcover edition as follows:

Owen, Carol, 1936-
  Crafting personal shrines :
using photos, mementos & treasures to create
artful displays / Carol Owen.
     p. cm.
  Includes bibliographical references and index.
  ISBN 1-57990-453-X
  1. Handicraft. 2. Household shrines. I. Title.
TT157.O85 2004
745.5--dc22

                                        2004006459

10 9 8 7 6 5 4 3 2

Published by Lark Books, A Division of
Sterling Publishing Co., Inc.
387 Park Avenue South, New York, N.Y. 10016

First Paperback Edition 2006
© 2004, Carol Owen

Distributed in Canada by Sterling Publishing,
c/o Canadian Manda Group, 165 Dufferin Street
Toronto, Ontario, Canada M6K 3H6

Distributed in the United Kingdom by GMC Distribution Services,
Castle Place, 166 High Street, Lewes, East Sussex, England BN7 1XU

Distributed in Australia by Capricorn Link (Australia) Pty Ltd.,
P.O. Box 704, Windsor, NSW 2756 Australia

If you have questions or comments about this book, please contact:
Lark Books
67 Broadway
Asheville, NC 28801
(828) 253-0467

Manufactured in China

ISBN 13: 978-1-57990-453-1 (hardcover) 978-1-57990-811-9 (paperback)
ISBN 10: 1-57990-453-x (hardcover) 1-57990-811-x (paperback)

For information about custom editions, special sales, premium and corporate purchases, please contact Sterling Special Sales Department at 800-805-5489 or specialsales@sterlingpub.com.

Contents

Introduction

Welcome to *Crafting Personal Shrines*. In this book you'll find everything you need to know, and then some, to help you construct and decorate a personal shrine. Using my simple construction techniques, you'll learn to make artful enclosures to capture whatever story you would like to tell: of travel, of someone special in your life, or of an event you want to celebrate or commemorate. You can make some-

thing meaningful to you using readily available materials and tools (such as foam board, paper and glue) and skills that are simple to master. I'm not a woodworker or metalsmith, so I had to come up with a way to build these shrines without methods beyond my abilities. My goal with this book is to show you how you can do the same, using your own photos and memorabilia to create an object that has both beauty and deep meaning for you.

When you look over the Getting Started chapter that follows, you will see that it's not just a list of supplies to purchase. I've packed it with lots of information about the kinds of things I use and why I use them. I think you'll find it will not only give you solid information about what is necessary to build a shrine, but it will spark your imagination, as well.

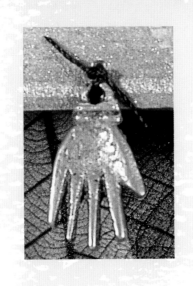

In How to Build a Shrine with Six Variations, you will discover clear step-by-step instructions for building the seven styles of shrine I most often use. The chapter begins with the fundamental structure which is then modified to create six distinct variations. That section is followed by Decorating Your Shrine with useful tips and techniques for decorating your creation; I've tested them all in my more-than-10 years as a shrine maker.

More hands-on techniques are discussed in A Maker's Dozen, a chapter that features the work of 12 contemporary shrine makers who not only display their work as inspiration, but also offer you essential, useful tips culled from experience. In this section and The Gallery that follows, you will discover that although the desire to create shrines is both timeless and universal, individual reasons for doing so—and ways of expressing that desire—vary widely and with much originality. The gallery features the work of amazing artists doing contemporary shrines. My hope is they will inspire you to come up with your own approach to making assemblages that tell your personal story.

Spirit houses along the kh'ong (canal) in Bangkok, Thailand. © MATT LEPKOWSKI, 2002. COURTESY OF TRAVELSINPARADISE.COM

A Personal Journey

My works are shrines to family memories. I wanted to explore more personal issues after doing mostly decorative art for many years as a landscape painter and a weaver. I had already started using old family photographs in some work with handmade paper. Then I learned about the spirit houses of Thailand from a friend who'd just visited there. She told me that every building has one of these small structures, and they are believed to protect the inhabitants from ill fortune. My assemblages grew from that conversation.

My shrines, which I also call spirit houses, are the logical extension of years of working with the house image. I had never really considered why the house held such meaning for me, yet most of my paintings have a house in them somewhere. Even when I was weaving, I did rooftop and village tapestries. I have collections of small ceramic and wooden houses, even jewelry with that theme. When I started making my own spirit houses, I realized that I'd lost a number of houses in my lifetime.

In a sense, I'm recapturing those lost homes. I am a nester; I joke that I put down roots at a long traffic light. For me, the house represents shelter and safety and family connections, something intensely personal and meaningful.

When I started this work, it was based on my own family; eventually I wanted a more universal vocabulary. The photographs and objects I use now are of imagined families, but they are no less real to me. In fact, I make up stories as I'm working. Recently, I put together a collage using an old wedding photograph of a couple, along with a postcard of a hotel in Paris, and a floor plan of

a house. I feel sure this couple had a wonderful honeymoon in France and came back to their first house. I hope they had a long and happy life together!

When I started exhibiting and selling my shrines, I discovered that people were very excited by the possibility of special-ordering one, to be made using their own photographs and memorabilia. Consequently, I have done commissions covering the whole range of life's experiences: to commemorate a marriage or a new baby, graduation from high school or college, anniversaries, and to celebrate retirement. I've done many shrines for special birthdays, includ-

ing the magical coming-of-age at 21; for a grandmother turning 100; and for lots of years in between. A mother brought me the record of her 18-year-old daughter's life saved in paper bags, one for each year. They were full of school papers, swim-meet ribbons, and birthday cards. The girl was about to go off to college and her mother wanted her to take her family with her. Another mother had me do one about her young daughter who died, and she gave me a boxful of her Girl Scout badges. I agonized about that commission, feeling the responsibility. Her thank-you letter made me cry because she said she felt as if I'd known her daughter personally, and I knew I'd really done something worthwhile. I also did one for a woman who was going into a nursing home; her daughter told me it had made her mother a real person to the staff. They all came into her room to look at the shrine, which had details about her mother's life as a nurse and an Outward Bound leader.

I feel privileged that people have let me into their lives this way. Now I'm teaching workshops and writing this book to help people make their own shrines. We all have special people and special moments in our lives that we want to celebrate and remember, and these assemblages are a wonderful way to do that.

"I am a nester; I joke that I put down roots at a long traffic light. For me, the house represents shelter and safety and family connections..."

A Universal Experience

So what is a shrine? The dictionary talks about a receptacle for sacred relics, or a place considered sacred because of its relationship to a holy person or event. That's the religious definition. Today, artists create shrines to express many different things, often not religious. They may be political, humorous, or satirical. They can be about family, travel, nature, or just about anything that interests the creator. They may express a strong emotion of the moment—anger or joy. They may contain a message or comment on everyday events, or be concerned with the same themes found in shrines from ancient times: mankind's relationship to the earth, and the mysteries of life and death.

By using the shrine format (objects in an enclosure of some sort), and enshrining objects of significance to them, the artist creates a window looking at what is personally important, showing that there is something here of greater meaning than just a pleasing composition or color scheme.

The making of shrines has long been part of the human experience. They date back to the beginning of recorded time and have been found most everywhere in the world. The earliest shrines we know of, dating from 7000 BCE, were discovered in what is now Turkey. In Greece, the Ukraine, and Moldavia, shrines from 5000-3500 BCE were found containing Mother Earth goddess figures. Fertility images were also common in the Celtic world.

Some themes are common to all ancient shrines, wherever and whenever they were made. They express the most basic human concerns: birth, life, and death. People used their shrines to ask for help in an unpredictable, harsh, and frightening world. In the past, the focus was often on survival, at a time when life depended on the whims of nature. Shrines were often important parts of holy sites where people made offerings to their gods, asking for protection against disease; for favorable weather; for successful crops; and for fertility for women and the land. A shrine was where people went to ask for help from the greater unseen powers that governed their lives. Shrines gave tangible form to belief.

For instance, the shrine to the god Apollo at Delphi was an important part of everyday life in ancient Greece. People went to Delphi seeking answers about their destiny from Apollo, the god of the sun and light. It was believed Apollo was a healer.

Columns of Temple of Apollo, CA. 366-329 BCE, in Delphi, Greece.
PHOTO, CA. 2001, © ROYALTY-FREE/CORBIS.

Greek shrine on dangerous mountain road from Tripolis to Argos, overlooking the bay toward Nafplio. PHOTO, 2002, BY PETER VAN ERP.

Family shrine in Vietnam. PHOTO, 1970, BY KENNETH HOFFMAN.

According to Greek legend, his son, Asclepius, became a physician, and was worshipped as the god of medicine. These myths carried into Roman culture, and the citizens built Asclepius a major shrine after the city of Rome survived a plague. Houses in ancient Rome contained shrines with images of the family's ancestors; this is where the residents made daily offerings to the household gods, to honor their ancestors, and to ask for protection for the family.

In New Mexico, in the southwestern United States, the tradition of household shrines continues to this day. It dates back 400 years to a time when the settlers were often far away from a church, and Catholic priests had to travel to remote areas to care for their parishioners. Private shrines at home helped the devout practice their faith while they were on their own.

In Japan, the Shinto sun goddess shrine at Ise dates back to the first century CE. Shinto ceremonies revolve around the gods of the sun, earth, and moon, and the gods of fertility are also revered. Today, private Shinto shrines are used for daily prayers for protection of the family, in much the same way Romans used their household shrines.

There are many countries in the world where we can see roadside shrines, some elaborate, some simple. Common in Greece, Poland, Mexico, Italy and Japan, for example, sometimes these shrines mark the spot of a fatal accident, to remember the dead. Sometimes they are dedicated to a saint or other religious figure and provide a place for a moment of prayer or meditation. Shrines can be private, in a house or yard, used by individuals or a family, or by a larger group. T'ai Shan is a sacred mountain in China where Buddhists have come since 2000 BCE. They climb the mountain on a path lined with many shrines to pay homage to their gods and to remember their ancestors.

When I read about these older customs, I feel that the purpose of my own work is not so very different. By exploring my past and honoring those who went before me, I am enriching my life, and passing on that legacy to those who come next. For example, I've used a spiral in my work ever since I learned that the Native American Hopi consider it a symbol for a journey. That image seems appropriate for the creation of these shrines because exploring personal history is a journey from the past to the present. The spiral also represents an inward journey of discovery, exploring feelings and memories of family. I am especially glad to be able to help others to explore their own history and tell their own story. I hope this book encourages you to acknowledge events and people important to you, to celebrate those things that matter in your life.

Getting Started

When I read how-to books I often skip this chapter. I'm too impatient and eager to jump right in. I'll glance over it to make sure it doesn't involve anything too exotic, and then I'll move on to the rest of the book, hoping to figure things out as I go. Sometimes that works out fine. Often, though, I discover that a very simple but essential piece of information I'd missed in the Getting Started section would have made things easier down the line. So in making that confession, I'm hoping to capture your attention for a few minutes, in order to save you some time and aggravation later on.

Supplies

Let me begin by talking about the basic tools and materials you'll need for building the structures for your personal shrines. You'll find there is nothing very strange or unusual. Many of the items you will have already, and others can be purchased at craft, art, or paper stores. If you do encounter any difficulty, you can find current information on locating these items by going to the Lark Books website at Larkbooks.com.

As you read, remember that these are the things I have found that work best for me. But as you get into this work, you might find a better implement or approach. My motto at all times is do whatever works for you.

Tools

• **Cutting mat** or something to cut on to protect your work surface. I use a self-healing cutting mat, found at quilting stores, large craft shops, or available by mail order. If you don't want to get one of these or can't find one, you can use heavy-duty cardboard, a piece of plywood, or a kitchen cutting board.

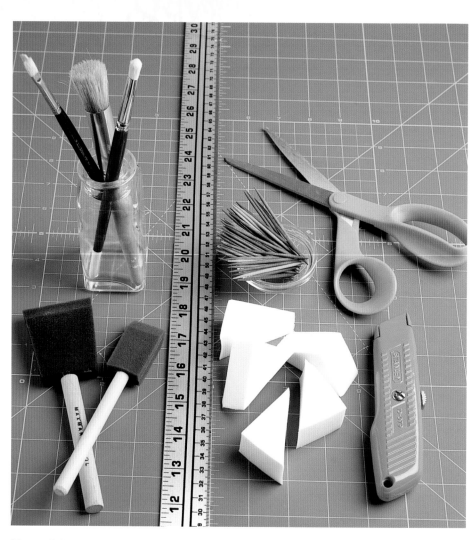

Many of the tools you will need may be found around the house. Others can be easily purchased from art, craft, or sewing stores.

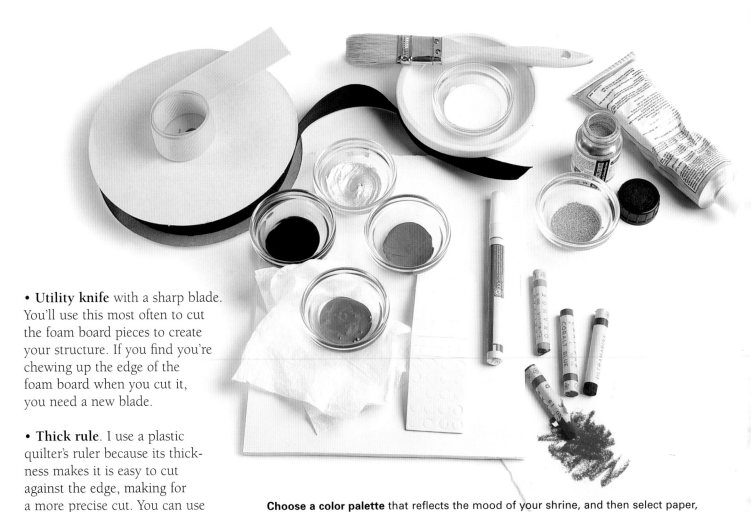

Choose a color palette that reflects the mood of your shrine, and then select paper, paints, and ribbon in those hues.

• **Utility knife** with a sharp blade. You'll use this most often to cut the foam board pieces to create your structure. If you find you're chewing up the edge of the foam board when you cut it, you need a new blade.

• **Thick rule**. I use a plastic quilter's ruler because its thickness makes it is easy to cut against the edge, making for a more precise cut. You can use a metal ruler if it helps give you an accurate cut.

• **Scissors**. Paper dulls scissors, so if you work with both fabric and paper, you'll want separate scissors for each.

• **Items for applying paint and glue**. Various sizes of brushes, sponges, small foam brushes and rollers, and toothpicks may be used. Little makeup sponges work great on small areas. I use ¾-inch (1.9 cm) and 1-inch (2.5 cm) wide brushes meant for acrylic paints to paint the body of shrines, and smaller brushes for detail work. I also use disposable foam brushes and little sponge rollers (found in the paint sections of hardware stores) for applying matte medium to the foam board. Often I use a toothpick to apply glue to small embellishment items.

Materials

• **Acrylic paints**. These may be found at art supply stores. Use your favorite colors or the ones that best tell your story. People respond to color emotionally; some colors make you sad, some make you happy, and some may remind you of your childhood. If you're doing a piece about your Great Aunt Matilda, you might want to use her favorite color or the color that reminds you of her house.

• **Linen tape**. Used for the door hinges; this may be found at art supply stores that carry bookmaking supplies or may be obtained by mail order. You can also use narrow grosgrain ribbon instead of linen tape. (If you want to avoid making hinges altogether, I'll show you how to make a shrine without a door in the how-to section.)

• **Matte medium**. Sold where you buy acrylic paints, it's used to thin acrylics but also works as an adhesive. It comes in both matte and gloss. I prefer to use the matte.

• **Foam board**. This is a sheet of rigid foam with paper on both sides. It is available in several thicknesses. I only use the ³⁄₁₆-inch (5mm) thickness, and recommend you not use anything thinner because it will be too flimsy. You can find it at art supply and craft stores.

Note: Foam board will warp unless you coat both sides with matte medium first. I cover one side with an undiluted layer of medium, using a brush or foam roller. When it's dry, I do the other side. You can do this before cutting the sheet, as I do, or you can coat the individual pieces with matte medium after you've cut them out. (This tip is your reward for reading this chapter. It will save you much trouble later on. If the pieces warp, it's almost impossible to glue them together properly.)

• **Glues**. Everyone seems to have personal favorites. I use a textile glue to attach all paper items. It's a white glue that dries flexible and clear. It sets up pretty quickly, but not instantly, so you have a little time to move things around if you change your mind during the process of assembling. White glues come in a whole range from school-grade quality to the glues used by professional book artists, so experiment with several to find one you like. For all embellishments not made of paper that have more dimension to them so need a stronger glue, I use a jewelry adhesive, which also dries quickly but not instantly. In addition, I like to use adhesive dots that come on a roll and are available in a few different sizes. They even come in a mini size, which is especially useful for attaching small items like buttons. Some artists use two-part epoxy gel. Experiment to find your own

favorites. From now on, I will refer to these two types of glue as paper glue or embellishment glue.

• **Japanese rice paper**. I use a type called Chiri, which has little flecks of bark in it. It's strong, but thin enough to give a crisp edge when I wrap it around the foam board. It takes paint beautifully. Tissue paper is too thin, but you can experiment to find another paper that might work well for you. You can get sheets of Japanese rice paper at art supply stores.

• **Metallic pens**, **oil pastels**, and **metallic powder**. I use these to add details such as outlines around doors or windows, or to highlight photographs, or to edge rooftop shingles.

Collage and Embellishment

It's great fun to comb through flea markets, antique shops (the junkier the better), estate sales, and yard sales for the distinctive small items which will give your work its particular character and tell your story. I never know what I might find, and that's part of the adventure, like going on a treasure hunt when you don't know exactly what you're looking for. I search for small items of the right scale for my work—things with an aura, a mystery to them. I ask myself questions: Does this item add to the story I'm trying to tell? Will it make the viewer wonder and imagine? Does it evoke memories

of a place or a time or an association with someone?

If you're telling your family story, you might have items at hand already. Everyone seems to have a drawer or box of little things they've collected. You feel you can't throw them out, but you don't know what to do with them. Well, now you know! I consider these things the vocabulary I use for my artwork.

Collage Materials

• **Old paper goods**. These are usually called ephemera in the antique business. I consider anything paper to be fair game, including scraps or fragments as well as larger pieces. I feel like I've found treasure when I come across ticket stubs, wedding or graduation announcements, old letters, school papers, envelopes, ledger sheets, playbills, and so forth. Once, in an antique store, I was delighted to find a wedding certificate from Russia from early in the 1900s. Often I'll make copies of these old documents instead of using the originals. Working with a copy allows you to cut or fold, and then if you change your mind, you can simply make another copy.

• **Old photographs**. I look for interesting and pleasant faces. Having your picture taken was serious stuff in the past and life was often hard. I've seen a lot of grim people and I pass those pictures up,

although you may find something evocative in such images. When I first started making shrines, they were just done for myself with my own family photographs. I gathered up some of my favorites and quickly realized I didn't want to tear them up or paint on them, so I made photocopies and have done so ever since. Most copy machines can enlarge or reduce images and can lighten or darken as well. Sometimes it takes a little fiddling to get an old photograph to reproduce well. You can also try photocopying black and white photographs on the color setting to get a wonderful sepia tone.

• **Decorative papers**, art papers, and interesting wrapping papers.

• **Sheet music**.

• **Postcards**.

• **School yearbooks**. I found a yearbook from 1918 with pictures and comments about the teachers, clippings of sporting events, and other school happenings. It was a real pot of gold for me.

• **Maps**. I have an old atlas and I photocopy particular states or parts of the world to tell the story I have in

mind. I've always been fascinated by maps. I particularly like interesting names of places that suggest their own stories, like Go Home in the Georgian Bay area of Ontario, Canada. I always wondered if the residents were telling visitors to leave, or if they were recent immigrants longing to go home themselves, wherever home might have been. Giving a title to my pieces is always difficult for me, and often I'll use a place name from a map I've used in that particular shrine.

• **Postage stamps**. I have a huge collection of old stamps from all over

them into my work, including using rubber stamps of these images. I use some that I've carved myself. Many rubber stamp companies have stamps of text, poetry, sayings, bits of ancient script, and the like, and I use many of these. I also have stamps with symbols on them such as a spiral or a hand. The hand is a protection and a blessing symbol in many cultures. An open hand signifies generosity of spirit to me.

• **Stencils**. These can be used in the same way as rubber stamps.

Embellishments

• **Buttons**. These common items are surprisingly evocative for most everybody. Often people tell me they remember playing with their mother's or grandmother's button box when they were children. I use buttons as a personal reference to my family's history in the garment industry. At a flea market I found a bag of military buttons from the Civil War and I use them as doorknobs or drawer pulls, creating stories about an ancestor in the war.

• **Bones**. These are meaningful to me because I collect them on our beach in Canada. They are beautiful pieces of miniature sculpture. After I boil them and bleach them to clean them up, I paint them with washes of acrylic paint to age them visually. Bones represent a specific place and time important to our family, but beyond that, bones are a reference to the past; they are a metaphor for the essence of life. I love to use them for all these reasons.

• **Shells**. Who can visit the beach and resist picking up handfuls? I look for shells that are the right size for my work, with interesting shapes or colors. Once on a trip to the English

the world. I like their decorative nature, but they are also references to trips taken and to the interests, hobbies, and geographical backgrounds of the subjects I'm working with. If I'm doing a commission, I'll search out stamps meaningful to that family.

• **Bits of antique lace**. A friend gave me a collection of old lace that her grandmother had with her when she escaped from Europe during World War II. My friend wasn't interested in

saving it any longer, and said she preferred to see it used in my artwork. I received it gratefully, even reverently, but of course that doesn't keep me from tearing it into little pieces for my shrines. I use textile glue to attach the lace, and then go over it with a little matte medium to seal and protect it.

• **Rubber stamps**. Numbers, letters, and texts fascinate me. There are many ways in which I incorporate

countryside with friends, we were walking through a field when I came across several small yellow snail shells. Every time I use one of them in a shrine, it reminds me of that walk.

• **Keys**. Again, another everyday object, but keys have layers of meaning for both the shrine maker and the viewer. Keys suggest unlocking secrets, keeping things safe, locking things away, finding treasure buried in the past, and " the key to my heart." I prefer using flat keys because they're easier to attach. If I use a round or thicker key, I'll often sew it on.

• **Items from nature** such as feathers, lichen, bits of bark, acorn caps, twigs, and pods. I go to an art summer camp in the mountains of California where I find huge armfuls of tumbleweed (a real challenge to get that home in my suitcase!), and segments of red pinecones just lying on the ground. I can't resist picking them up. The tumbleweed has a wonderful bleached cream color. After trimming off the feathery tops (no way can I get those parts home), I use the twigs as fence posts or pillars in my shrines.

• **Reeds** for musical instruments. I come home from that same art camp with another item, manmade rather than from nature—bassoon reeds. A professional musician with a chamber music orchestra often attends my class and presents us with his old reeds, wonderfully painted and decorated. I use them in my work because they remind me of those classes, and especially because the reeds are mysterious objects to most people. I get all kinds of guesses about what they are, and only people familiar with wind instruments guess right. Viewers get lost in the details of my shrines, and I enjoy engaging them this way.

• **Shark's teeth**. After seeing the kinds of things I was using, my son gave me his collection, and I love using them, both for their interesting shapes and because he gave them to me.

• **Small spoons**, such as baby spoons and commemorative spoons. I find them at flea markets and antique shows. In the same ways that buttons and keys are meaningful, so are spoons. They remind me of family dinners at my grandmother's. She was a wonderful cook, but she always for-

got at least one dish still sitting in the oven or refrigerator until the meal was finished when she would discover it. She was always furious with herself. She was so busy serving everyone she never sat down to eat with us, and the whole time she was giving us great food, she would complain it hadn't come out right. I think of these stories when I look at the spoons I've collected. I use souvenir spoons because they have place names or historical events inscribed on them and are memories of family trips.

• **Game pieces**. At an estate sale I came across a complete set of mah-jongg tiles. They sent me back to my childhood when my mother played with her friends. They're the perfect size to use as doorsteps, or used standing on their side they suggest fences. I use dominoes the same way. Scrabble tiles are a wonderful way to incorporate letters and words into a shrine, and bingo cards can provide both letters and numbers.

• **Antique measuring tape**. I found a large roll of old tape at my favorite flea market. It's pretty grungy and much used, but to age it even further, I tear off pieces to get a ragged edge, paint them, and sand them. I use them to outline various parts of the shrines, such as the windows or around the base.

• **Rusty nails**. These suggest old houses to me. I use them in fetish bundles. I combine a nail, a bone, a twig of tumbleweed, or a sprig of lavender or rosemary, then wrap it in a bit of old lace or scrap of paper and tie it up with thread embellished with a bead. Native American fetishes inspired these little bundles, and I use them as symbols for protecting family memories, the essence of my work.

• **Beads, charms** and **milagros**. Charms may be found in antique stores, but also in bead shops. I use hearts, stars, fish, birds, flowers, hands, and anything else I find that intrigues me. Milagros are small metal religious charms used as prayer objects for healing, and can be found in stores that have Mexican imports, in the southwest U. S. and from sources online.

• **Baby blocks** and **jacks**. These are reminiscent of childhood, and the blocks may also contain letters or pictures.

• **Costume jewelry**, watch parts, and cuff links. All those mismatched earrings and old pendants, broken watches, and cuff links no longer worn now have a place and a purpose.

• **Coins** and **medals**. They are just the right size and full of meaning.

Often the things people give me to use in commissions are a real challenge, and pose an interesting problem to solve. Someone asked me to do a piece for his wife as a birthday surprise. He gave me an assortment of her childhood costume jewelry that her mother had been saving for years. I had a lot of fun with that shrine, figuring out how best to use the various pieces. The barrettes made wonderful drawer pulls. Someone else gave me her daughter's award ribbons from swim meets and I layered them for the rooftop shingles. It's a fun and creative part of the process to find an object and try to figure out how it can be used cleverly. This should give you an idea of the kinds of things I use, but I'm sure you will come up with many more ideas of your own.

How to Build a Shrine
with Six Variations

Shrine One

Tools

Utility knife

Cutting mat

Ruler

Pencil

Paper clips or bookmaker's bone folder (optional)

Straight pins or string

Materials

Matte medium

Foam board [1 board, approximately 22 x 28 inches (56 x 71 cm), is sufficient]

White or cream-colored rice paper, approximately 23 x 35 inches (58 x 89 cm). (Note: Rice paper comes in many different sizes. If you have paper you want to use in other sizes, you can adjust the amounts you need accordingly. You will be cutting the sheets of paper, and some of the pieces you will cut out are small. It's possible, then, that you can use several small sheets of paper rather than the single large one directed here.)

Paper glue and embellishment glue

Acrylic paints

Collage and embellishment materials

Note: Instead of cutting the foam board pieces all at one time, I cut and assemble the shrine one piece at a time. This allows me to measure as I go for greatest accuracy in fitting the pieces together. I have learned that it's easy to be off by a little bit, and a mistake with an early piece will throw off those that follow.

Shrine One

In the instructions for the following seven structures, the first is the easiest to build and forms the base for the others.

Instructions

1 Coat both sides of the foam board with matte medium to prevent warping. Allow to dry.

The Back Wall and Roof

2 To make the back wall, mark a 5 x 9-inch (13 x 23 cm) rectangle on a piece of foam board. Use a cutting mat to protect your work surface. With a sharp utility knife, cut the rectangle. (To cut through evenly, do it in two or three strokes, cutting deeper with each pass. Keep the blade perpendicular to the work surface.) Photo 1 shows the stages of this process.

DIMENSIONS

The finished size
of Shrine One is 9½ inches high x 5½ inches wide x 2¼ inches deep (24 x 14 x 6 cm).

The dimensions
of the foam board pieces are as follows:
Back wall, 5 x 9 inches (13 x 28 cm)
Ceiling, 5 x 1½ inches (13 x 4 cm)
Side walls (2), 6 ¾ x 1½ inches (17 x 4 cm)
Floor, 4½ x 1½ inches (11 x 4 cm)
Frame, 5 x 7 inches (13 x 18 cm)
Roof, 6½ x 2 inches (16 x 5 cm)
Base, 5½ x 2¼ inches (14 x 6 cm)

Photo 1

Photo 2

3 Mark the center point along the top, short side of the rectangle. This will be the peak of the roof. Make a mark 2 inches (5 cm) down from the top on each long side and use a ruler to make pencil lines from the peak point at the top to each of these side points. Cut along this line, creating a triangular end to your rectangle.

4 Cut a piece of rice paper large enough to wrap around both sides of the back wall, with approximately a ¼-inch (.6 cm) margin on all sides. (This does not need to be a precise measurement. The paper should just cover the foam board edges. You can do it by sight, and if you've left too much paper, trim it as you're gluing.)

5 Brush paper glue on one side of the foam board and position it along one edge of the paper, leaving approximately ¼-inch (.6 cm) of margin along that side, along the bottom and above the peak point. Gently smooth the paper, pressing out any air bubbles or wrinkles. Cut away the excess triangles of paper to make the paper match the peak of the roof, again leaving approximately ¼-inch margin.(See photo 2.)

6 Put a small amount of glue along both long edges, and fold the margin of paper up along these edges. (See photo 3.)

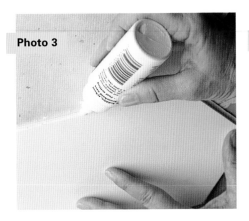
Photo 3

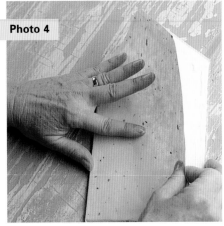
Photo 4

Note: The glues I use come with a nozzle tip, and I drizzle the glue onto the surface of the foam board or paper. If you want a more even application, you can use a brush. It's helpful to keep a few damp paper towels near your work area to wipe glue off your fingers. I'm a messy worker and always seem to be covered with paint and glue. I keep a jar of water handy for cleaning off brushes, and if I'm in a fever of creation, I'm apt to stick my fingers into the jar of mucky water to clean them. Paper towels work better!

7 Put glue on the other side of the foam board, and again smooth the paper. (See photo 4.)

8 Fold over the ¼-inch (.6 cm) margin of paper and glue it down onto the edge. Do the same with the remaining margins of paper along the bottom and the triangle of the roof. (It's like wrapping a package. You fold the ends in first and then the longer pieces. When dealing with the peak of the roof, do one side at a time, folding in the ends first.) (See photos 5 and 6.)

Photo 5

The Ceiling

9 To make the ceiling, cut a piece of foam board 5 inches (13 cm) long x 1½ inches (4 cm) wide. Measure the actual width of your back wall before cutting the 5-inch length, and adjust the size if need be to make sure they match exactly.

10 Cover the ceiling piece with paper, just as you did with the back wall.

11 Put a line of glue along one long edge of the ceiling piece and glue it exactly where the attic triangle begins. The top of the ceiling should not extend above this point. (See photo 7.)

Note: The 1½-inch (4 cm) width of the ceiling piece determines the depth of your shrine, but it can be as deep as you like. Mine are usually 1½ or 2 inches (4 or 5 cm) unless I need more depth to accommodate an embellishment that needs more space.

Photo 6

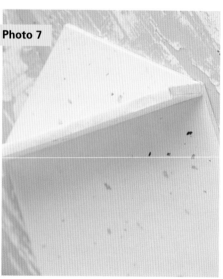

Photo 7

The Side Walls

12 To make the side walls, cut two pieces of foam board 6¾ x 1½ inches (17 x 4 cm) each. Again, to be sure of the actual size needed, measure down from the ceiling to the bottom of the back wall and adjust your measurement accordingly.

13 Cover these two pieces with paper as you have been doing.

14 Glue each side wall to a long side of the back wall. (They sit atop the back wall and their top edges fit snugly under the ceiling.) (See figure 1.)

The Floor

15 To make the floor, cut a piece of foam board 4½ x 1½ inches (11 x 4 cm).

16 Cover this piece with paper as you have been doing.

17 Glue the floor piece between the side walls at the bottom of the back wall. (See photo 8)

The Frame

18 To make the frame that goes in front of the shrine, measure and cut a rectangle 5 x 7 inches (13 x 18 cm). Again, check the measurements of your shrine and adjust these to make sure it will be an exact fit.

19 To make the opening in this frame, measure ¾ inch (2 cm) in from the edge all the way around and use the utility knife to cut this piece out. (See photo 9.)

Photo 8

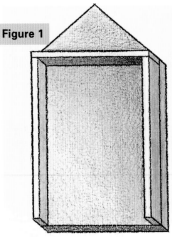
Figure 1

Photo 9

20 Before you cover this frame with paper, you will want to cover the inner corners of the window you just created (see photo 9.) To do this, make tabs from four small pieces of rice paper, each one approximately 1¼ x 1 inch (3 x 2.5 cm). Make two slits in each one, on either side [across the width, leaving ¼ inch (.6 cm) uncut. Make sure you don't cut all the way across]. Glue one in each inner corner of the frame. The slits allow you to fold the paper neatly over the edges. (See figure 2.)

Note: I worked out these procedures through trial and error. When I made my first shrine, I assembled the whole structure, then realized how difficult it would be to cover it neatly with paper afterwards. Now I cover each piece of foam board first and then assemble the shrine. The first time I constructed a frame for the front, I was left with raw inner corners, so I came up with these paper tabs as a way to cover them.

21 Cut a piece of paper approximately 1 inch (2.5 cm) larger than the frame on all sides. You want it big enough to wrap around to the back, but since only one side of the frame shows, the paper doesn't have to fully cover the back side.

22 Brush glue on the front of the frame and center it on the paper.

Photo 10

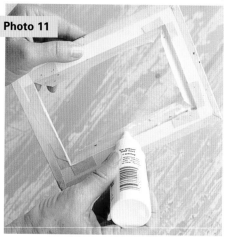

Photo 11

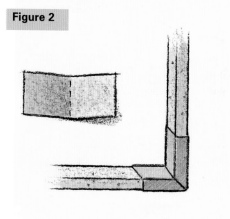

Figure 2

23 Working with one side of the frame at a time, put glue on the edges, fold the paper over and glue it to the back, folding the excess paper in at the ends.

24 With the frame facedown, cut away the paper covering the inner window, leaving enough of a margin [approximately ½ inch (1.25 cm)] to cover the edges when you fold the paper to the back.

25 Cut a diagonal slit from the inner corners of the paper up to the corners of the frame. (See photo 10.) Fold the paper over and glue it to the back. (See photo 11.) Photo 12 shows the completed frame. Do not glue it to the main body of the shrine yet; wait until you have decorated the interior of the shrine.

The Decorations

26 Now paint the whole shrine, inside and out, as well as the frame. The frame can be the same color as the rest or a contrasting color. I use acrylic paints, either from the tube (diluted) or fluid acrylics in bottles.

Note: It's not necessary to paint the entire interior of the shrine if you know you're going to cover it up with a collage of paper, for instance. However, I never know ahead of time exactly where I'm going to put things, so it's easier to paint everything in the beginning than it is to worry about covering up raw spots later.

27 At this point you will want to decorate the interior of your shrine with collage and embellish it. Please see the section on Decorating Your Shrine on page 52.

28 After decorating the interior, attach the frame by gluing it to the rim of the shrine. Make sure it fits evenly all the way around, especially making sure that the bottom edge of the frame is flush with the bottom of the shrine; otherwise, you won't have a flat surface when you attach it to the base in the final step. (See photo 13.)

Photo 12

Photo 13

Photo 14

The Roof

29 To make the roof, cut a piece of foam board 2¼ x 7 inches (6 x 18 cm).

30 Lightly score a line across the middle, being careful not to cut all the way through. (See photo 14.) (You can use the rounded edge of a paper clip to make this score line, or a pencil that's not too sharp, or the tip of a bookmaker's bone folder if you have one.)

31 Cover the roof piece with paper and paint it. I usually use a contrasting color to the color of the shrine.

32 Gently bend the roof along the scored line. It won't break. (See photo 15.)

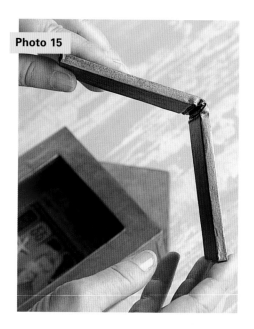

Photo 15

33 Glue the roof to the edges of the attic triangle and to the side edges of the ceiling. The ends of the roof will extend beyond the side walls. (See photo 16.)

Note: To help the roof stay in place while the glue is drying, you can pin it in place with straight pins (remove the pins later), or you can tie string or ribbon around the whole house and roof and let it dry overnight.

34 When the glue has dried and the roof is securely in place, cover the roof with collage. I use pieces of maps, photos, sheet music, or other ephemera.

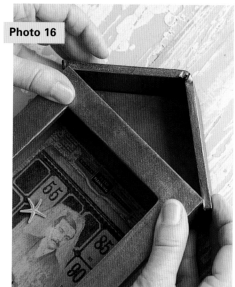

Photo 16

The Base

35 Shrine One has a flat base, made from a single piece of foam board. To make this base, cut a piece of foam board 2¼ x 5 inches (6 x 13 cm). Cover with paper and paint.

36 Glue the shrine to the base. (See photo 17.)

Note: The base of your shrine can be larger, if you like. I usually make the base extend at least ¼ inch (.6 cm) on either side of the shrine and ½ inch (1.3 cm) beyond the front.

This completes Shrine One.
The following shrines use the same basic techniques: the cutting of the foam board, covering with paper, and painting are the same.

Photo 17

Shrine Two

Shrine Two

Shrine Two has a hinged door that fits into the frame, and an open box base that forms a niche (a perfect place for an embellishment).

Tools

Utility knife

Cutting mat

Ruler

Pencil

Paper clips or bookmaker's bone folder (optional)

Straight pins or string

Materials

Matte medium

Foam board [1 board, approximately 22 x 28 inches (56 x 71 cm), is sufficient]

White or cream-colored rice paper, approximately 23 x 35 inches (58 x 89 cm). (Note: Rice paper comes in many different sizes. If you have paper you want to use in other sizes, you can adjust the amounts you need accordingly. You will be cutting the sheets of paper, and some of the pieces you will cut out are small. It's possible, then, that you can use several small sheets of paper rather than the single large one directed here.)

Paper glue and embellishment glue

Acrylic paints

Linen tape or narrow ribbon, approximately 4 inches (10 cm) long and ¼ inch (.6 cm) wide

Collage and embellishment materials

Instructions

Making adjustments for the changed dimensions in the pieces for Shrine Two, follow the directions for Shrine One through step 19, the point where you cut out the inner part of the frame. For Shrine Two, the piece you cut out will become the door.

1 To make this door, cut off a thin sliver from one long edge and one short edge [approximately ¹⁄₁₆ inch (.16 cm) from each] from the cut-out piece to ensure it will open and close easily.

2 Cover both sides of the door with paper and paint it. I use a color that contrasts with the frame, but that's your choice.

3 To make hinges for the door, use linen tape or narrow ribbon. Cut four pieces, each about 1 inch (2.5 cm) long.

4 Glue the end of one piece of tape to the front of the door on the long side, about ½ inch (1.3 cm) down from the top of the door. On the back of the door, glue the end of another piece, just under the piece on the front. When folded over the edge, they should just clear each other. (See figure 1.) Do the same with the remaining two pieces of tape near the bottom of the door:

Figure 1

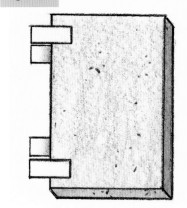

Photo 1

Shrine Two with door open

one piece glues to the front and one to the back, starting about ½ inch (1.3 cm) up from the bottom. Make sure they clear each other when folded over the edge. (See photo 1.) Do not put glue on the middle part of the hinge!

5 Fold the front tapes to the back, and the back tapes to the front. Set the door into the frame. (See photo 2.)

6 Glue the ends of the back tapes to the front of the frame. When the glue is dry, carefully turn the whole piece over (frame and door) and glue the ends of the front tapes to the back of the frame. (See photo 3.)

7 When the door and frame are assembled, add a door handle. Select a bead, button, or other dimensional embellishment and attach it with embellishment glue.

Note: In the shrine pictured, I used a coin for a door pull. By gluing only half of the coin to the door and letting the rest of the coin extend onto the frame, you can keep the door from swinging inside the shrine. Or you can create a doorstop for the same purpose. To make a doorstop, see the directions in Shrine Six, step 7, page 47.

Photo 2

Photo 3

8 Add the roof as described in the directions for Shrine One, steps 29-34, page 26.

9 To construct the box base pictured in Shrine Two, cut two pieces of foam board 3½ x 6 inches (9 x 15 cm) for the top and bottom pieces and cover both pieces with paper.

10 To make the back wall of the base, cut a piece of foam board 6 x 1½ inches (15 x 4 cm), cover with paper, and glue to the back of the bottom piece. (The back wall sits on top of the bottom piece.)

11 Cut two pieces for the sides 1½ x 3¼ inches (4 x 8 cm). These side pieces must be the same

height as the back piece and extend to the front of the base. Cover with paper and glue along the sides of the bottom piece. (See photo 4.)

12 Glue the top in place and paint the base inside and out. Glue the shrine onto the base, and using embellishment glue, put something interesting in the niche you've just created. (See photo 5.)

Photo 4

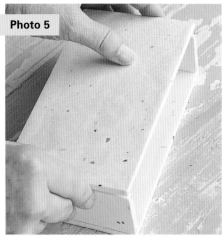

Photo 5

Shrine Three

Shrine Three

Shrine Three has a door with a window in it, and the door attaches directly to the shrine without a frame. A drawer fits in the niche in the base.

Tools

Utility knife

Cutting mat

Ruler

Pencil

Paper clips or bookmaker's bone folder (optional)

Straight pins or string

Materials

Matte medium

Foam board [1 board, approximately 22 x 28 inches (56 x 71 cm), is sufficient]

White or cream-colored rice paper, approximately 23 x 35 inches (58 x 89 cm). (Note: Rice paper comes in many different sizes. If you have paper you want to use in other sizes, you can adjust the amounts you need accordingly. You will be cutting the sheets of paper, and some of the pieces you will cut out are small. It's possible, then, that you can use several small sheets of paper rather than the single large one directed here.)

Paper glue & embellishment glue

Acrylic paints

Linen tape or narrow ribbon, approximately 4 inches (10 cm) long and ¼ inch (.6 cm) wide

Strong decorative paper, approximately 6 inches (15 cm) x 2 inches (5 cm)

Collage and embellishment materials

Instructions

1 Follow the directions for Shrine One but do not make the frame for the outside, which begins at Step 18. Instead, cut a piece of foam board to make the door to the exact dimensions of the front of the house, less ¼ inch (.6 cm) on one long side.

2 Measure and mark the size window you want and cut it out. [The one pictured is 2¼ x 3¼ inches (6 x 8 cm) and is 1 inch (2.5 cm) from the top and ¾ inches (1.9 cm) from each side.] Don't forget to cover the inner corners of this window with paper tabs, as explained in Shrine 1, step 20, page 24.

3 Cover the door with a piece of paper large enough to wrap around both sides.

4 Cut the paper away from the back of the window, being careful not to cut through to the front. Cut the paper flush with the edge of the opening. (Hold the door up to a light so you can see where the window is, slide the tip of your scissors just through the back piece of paper and cut out the rectangle.) Now cut the paper away that covers the front of the window, leaving about a ½-inch (1.3 cm) margin.

5 Cut diagonal slits up to the corners of the window, and glue the paper to the back of the door.

Note: Normally, I paint the house and door before I attach them, but for the purposes of these directions, I've left them unpainted in the photograph so you can see the details more clearly.

Photo 1

Photo 2

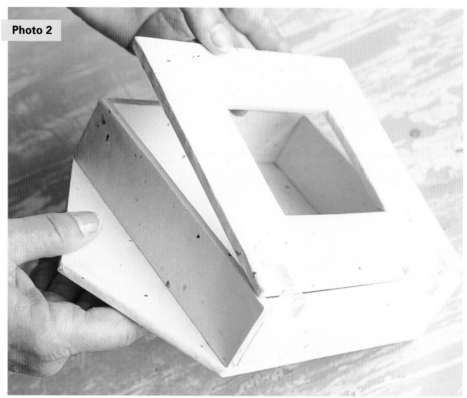

Figure 1

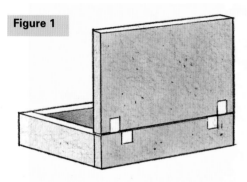

6 For the hinges, glue the four pieces of tape or ribbon to the door as explained in Shrine Two, steps 3-6, pages 29-30.

7 Attach the long edge of the door (the side with the hinges) to one edge of the shrine (See photo 1.), following the subsequent directions described in Shrine Two with this difference: Glue the tapes on the back of the door to the outside wall of the shrine, and the tapes from the front of the door to the inside wall. Do this with the shrine lying flat on its back and the door standing up with the long edge (with the hinges) flush against the long edge of the shrine. (See figure 1.)

8 When the door is attached and closed, it will leave a gap where the hinged side attaches to the shrine. You can cover this gap with a piece of strong decorative paper running down the edge with the hinges, and extending approximately 1 inch (2.5 cm) on either side, 1 inch on the door side, and 1 inch on the side wall.

Figure 2

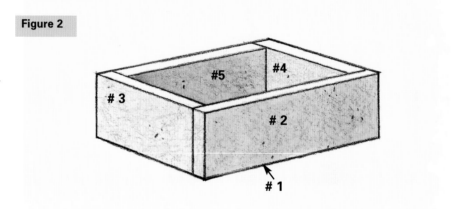

You can paint this strip of paper the same color as the shrine to make it less obtrusive, or you can accent it with another color. (See photo 2.)

Note: This shrine contains a drawer that fits in the niche in the base. It's important to make the drawer slightly smaller in all dimensions than the niche so it will open and close easily. (I learned this the hard way when I built a drawer to the exact size of the niche, and it was too tight to fit the space). I have numbered the pieces of the drawer in figure 2 to make the directions clearer: #1 is the bottom of the drawer, #2 is the front, #3 and #4 are the sides, and #5 is the back.

9 For the bottom piece, #1, cut a piece of foam board a little less than 8 x 2½ inches (20 x 7 cm) and cover with paper.

10 For the front, #2, cut a piece of foam board a little less than 8 inches long and a little less than 1½ inches wide (20 x 4 cm). Cover with paper.

Photo 3

Photo 4

buttons, cuff links, typewriter keys, game pieces, etc. Anything with a little dimension to it will work. You can attach these things with embellishment glue; or wire them on; or sew them, as I did here.

Note: To sew something to foam board, make holes in the board with an awl or an embroidery needle. Use a strong thread such as carpet thread, embroidery floss, or waxed linen.

15 Embellish the attic space and collage the rooftop.

Note: To make sure the door opens properly, the roof should be wide enough to cover the attic and the side walls but not the door.

11 Glue one long edge of #1 to the front piece, #2. (See photo 3.) To get a neater look, attach the front to the edge of the bottom piece instead of having it sit on top of the bottom piece. At this point, the bottom piece is flat and the front is standing up.

12 Cut side pieces #3 and #4 to the exact width of #1 and ¼ inch (.6 cm) less than the height of #2. Cover with paper, and glue in place, attaching the edges of #3 and #4 to the back of #2.

13 Now you can measure between the sides to know exactly what size piece to cut for the back wall. Cover the back, #5, with paper, and glue it between the sides and on top of #1. (See photo 4.)

14 Paint the finished drawer and give it a nifty drawer pull. For the shrine pictured, I used a wooden bobbin, and since it was so long and thin, I sewed it in place to make sure it stayed secure. I have used all kinds of things for drawer pulls: beads,

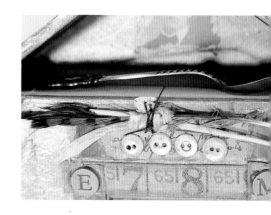

Shrine Four

Shrine Four

This shrine has a base with a center niche between two side panels.

Tools

Utility knife

Cutting mat

Ruler

Pencil

Paper clips or bookmaker's bone folder (optional)

Straight pins or string

Materials

Matte medium

Foam board [1 board, approximately 22 x 28 inches (56 x 71 cm), is sufficient]

White or cream-colored rice paper, approximately 23 x 35 inches (58 x 89 cm). (Note: Rice paper comes in many different sizes. If you have paper you want to use in other sizes, you can adjust the amounts you need accordingly. You will be cutting the sheets of paper, and some of the pieces you will cut out are small. It's possible, then, that you can use several small sheets of paper rather than the single large one directed here.)

Paper glue and embellishment glue

Acrylic paints

Linen tape or narrow ribbon, approximately 4 inches (10 cm) long and ¼ inch (.6 cm) wide

Strong decorative paper, approximately 8 inches (20 cm) x 2 inches (5 cm)

Collage and embellishment materials

Instructions

1 Construct the shrine as described in Shrine Three, (omitting the window in the door), up until step 9, page 34, when you begin to make the drawer that fits into the base.

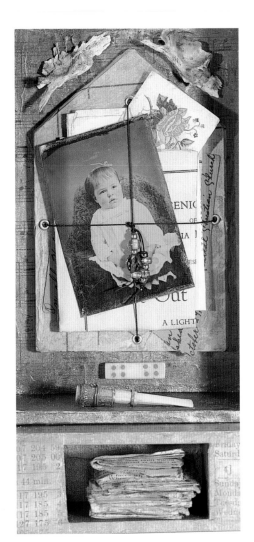

DIMENSIONS

The finished size
of Shrine Four is 12 inches high x 6 inches wide x 3 inches deep (30 x 15 x 7.5 cm)

The dimensions
of the foam board pieces are as follows:
Back wall: 5½ x 10 inches (14 x 25.5 cm)
Ceiling: 5½x 2 inches (14 x 5 cm)
Side walls (2): 7¾ x 2 inches (19.5 x 5 cm)
Floor: 5 x 2 inches (13 x 5 cm)
Roof: 8 x 2¼ inches (20 x 6 cm)
Door: 8 x 5¼ inches (20 x 13.5 cm)
Top and bottom pieces for the base: 6 x 3 inches (15 x 4 cm)
Back wall: 6 x 1½ inches (15 x 4 cm)
Side walls (2): 2¾ x 1½ inches (7 x 4 cm)
Front walls (2): 1½ x 1½ inches (4 x 4 cm)
Interior walls of the niche (2): 1¾ x 1½ inches (4.5 x 4 cm)
Interior back wall: 6 x 1½ inches (15 x 4 cm)

2 Construct the box base (this is the same as described in Shrine Two, steps 9-12, pages 30-31) by cutting out the bottom piece, the back wall, and the two sides from foam board, covering each with paper and gluing all these pieces together. Cut two pieces for the front panels, cover with paper, and glue them on either side up against the side walls. These pieces must be the same height as the side walls, but no higher, or the top won't fit flush.

Interior of Shrine Four

Photo 1

Photo 2

3 Cut the two pieces of foam board for the inner walls of the niche the same height as the side walls. Cover with paper and glue in place up against the front panels, one on either side. Photo 1 shows you a top view of this construction.

4 Make an inner back wall to prevent the drawer from going in too far. To make this inner wall, cut a piece of foam board the same width as the inside of the base and as high as the side walls, and cover with paper. Glue this inner back wall inside the base, up against the back edges of the interior walls, between the side walls. (See photo 2.)

5 Attach the top onto the base, paint it, and glue it to the shrine. (See photo 3.)

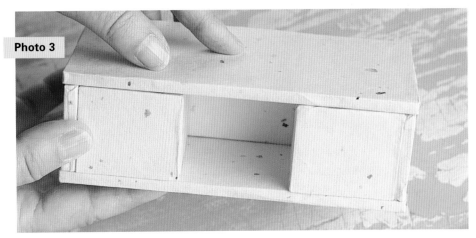

Photo 3

Shrine Five

Shrine Five

*This shrine has a door that attaches to a jamb
and has two niches and a drawer in the base.*

Tools

Utility knife

Cutting mat

Ruler

Pencil

Paper clips or bookmaker's
bone folder (optional)

Straight pins or string

Materials

Matte medium

Foam board [1 board, approximately 22 x 28 inches
(56 x 71 cm), is sufficient]

White or cream-colored rice
paper, approximately 23 x 35
inches (58 x 89 cm). (Note: Rice
paper comes in many different
sizes. If you have paper you want
to use in other sizes, you can
adjust the amounts you need
accordingly. You will be cutting
the sheets of paper, and some of
the pieces you will cut out are
small. It's possible, then, that you
can use several small sheets of
paper rather than the single large
one directed here.)

Paper glue and
embellishment glue

Acrylic paints

Linen tape or narrow ribbon,
approximately 4 inches (10 cm)
long and $\frac{1}{4}$ inch (.6 cm) wide

Collage and embellishment
materials

Instructions

Making adjustments for the changed
dimensions in Shrine Five, follow the
directions for Shrine One up to step
19, page 23.

1 To make the door for this shrine,
cut a piece of foam board to
the exact dimensions of the front
of the house.

2 Mark off 1 inch (2.5 cm) along
one long side. This 1-inch strip
will be the doorjamb, and the larger
piece will be the door. (See photo 1.)
Cut off the 1-inch strip and cover
both pieces with paper. Paint both
pieces now because it is easier to
paint them before they're attached.

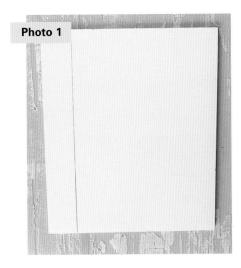

Photo 1

DIMENSIONS

The finished size
of Shrine Five is
11½ inches high x 7 inches wide
x 3¼ inches deep
(29 x 18 x 8 cm)

The dimensions
of the foam board pieces are as follows:
Back wall, 6 x 9 inches (15 x 23 cm)
Ceiling, 6 x 2 inches (15 x 5 cm)
Side walls (2), 7 x 2 inches (18 x 5 cm)
Floor, 5½ x 2 inches (14 x 5 cm)
Front, 6 x 7 inches (15 x 18 cm)
Roof, 8 x 2¼ inches (20 x 6 cm)
Top and bottom pieces of the base (2),
7 x 3¼ inches (18 x 8 cm)
Back wall of the base,
7 x 1¾ inches (18 x 4.5 cm)
Side walls (2), 3 x 1¾ inches
(7.5 x 4.5 cm)
Inner walls of the niche (cut 2),
1¾ x 1¾ inches (4.5 x 4.5 cm)
Interior back wall, 6½ x 1¾ inches
(16 x 4.5 cm)
Bottom of the drawer,
2⅞ x 1½ inches (7 x 4 cm)
Front of the drawer, 2⅞ inches (7 cm)
by less than 1¾ inches (4.5 cm)
Side walls of the drawers (2), 1½ x 1½
inches (4 x 4 cm) (I suggest you glue
the front to the bottom and then
measure to determine the exact
dimensions you will need for the sides.)
Back wall of the drawer,
2⅜ x 1½ inches (6.5 x 4 cm)

Interior of Shrine Five

Photo 2

3 Hinge the door to the jamb as explained in Shrine Two, steps 3-6, pages 29-30. (See photo 3.)

4 Collage the inside of the shrine.

5 Glue the jamb to the front of the shrine. Make sure you don't put glue on the door. You don't want to glue the door shut!

Note: The base for this shrine has three niches. A drawer fits into the center niche. The two side niches have interior walls that are flush with the front edge.

6 On the bottom of the base, mark off either side of where you want the drawer to go.

7 Cut two pieces the height of the side walls and as deep as you want the niches to be, cover with paper, and glue along the marked lines.

8 Put in an inner back wall, as described in Shrine Four, step 4, page 39. (See photo 4.)

9 Glue on the top of the base, paint it and glue to the shrine. (See photo 5.)

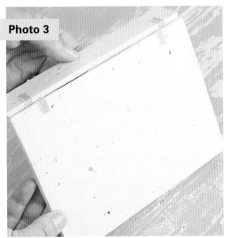

Photo 3

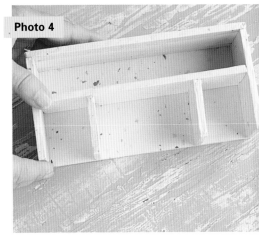

Photo 4

Photo 5

Shrine Six

Shrine Six

Shrine Six has double doors and niches on either side of the doors.

Tools

Utility knife

Cutting mat

Ruler

Pencil

Paper clips or bookmaker's bone folder (optional)

Straight pins or string

Materials

Matte medium

Foam board [2 boards, approximately 22 x 28 inches (56 x 71 cm), are sufficient]

White or cream-colored rice paper (2 sheets), approximately 23 x 35 inches (58 x 89 cm). (Note: Rice paper comes in many different sizes. If you have paper you want to use in other sizes, you can adjust the amounts you need accordingly. You will be cutting the sheets of paper, and some of the pieces you will cut out are small. It's possible, then, that you can use several small sheets of paper rather than the 2 larger ones directed here.)

Paper glue and embellishment glue

Acrylic paints

Linen tape or narrow ribbon, approximately 8 inches (20 cm) long and ¼ inch (.6 cm) wide

Collage and embellishment materials

Instructions

1 Construct this shrine as explained in Shrine One through step 17, page 23 .

2 Mark the place where the interior walls will go, 2½ inches (6.5 cm) in from the sides. The interior walls are the same depth as the side walls. Cover with paper and glue along the line you marked.

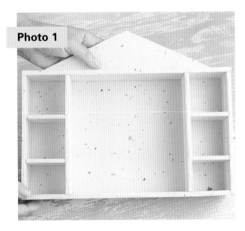

Photo 1

3 The shelves for the niches are cut to fit the depth and width of the space you've just created. Determine where you want the shelves to be, cover with paper and glue in place. Paint the whole shrine. (See photo 1.)

DIMENSIONS

The finished size
of Shrine Six is 12¾ inches high x 11 inches wide x 3¼ inches deep (32 x 28 x 7.7 cm).

The dimensions
of the foam board pieces are as follows:
Back wall, 11 x 13½ inches (28 x 34 cm)
Ceiling, 11 x 2 inches (28 x 5 cm)
Side walls (2), 11 x 2 inches (28 x 5 cm)
Floor, 10½ x 2 inches (26 x 5 cm)
Interior walls (2), 11 x 2 inches (28 x 5 cm)
Roof, 13 x 2¼ inches (33 x 6 cm)
Front of shrine, 6 x 11 inches (15 x 28 cm)
Shelves (4), 2 x 2 inches (5 x 5 cm) each
Top and bottom of the base, 12 x 3¼ inches (30 x 8 cm) each
Back wall of the base, 12 x 1½ inches (30 x 4 cm)
Side walls of the base (2), 3¼ x 1½ inches (8 x 4 cm)
Front panels of base (2), 1 x 1½ inch (2.5 x 4 cm)
Interior walls of niche in base (2), 1 x 1½ inch (2.5 x 4 cm)
Inner back wall, 12 x 1½ inches (30 x 4 cm)

Interior of Shrine Six

4 A frame covers the central part of Shrine Six and holds double doors. To determine the size of the frame, measure across the central part of the shrine from one inner wall of the niches to the other inner wall and from the ceiling to the floor. The frame will attach to these inner walls, so make sure the piece will just cover them.

5 Cut the measured frame out of foam board.

6 The next steps are the same as creating the door for Shrine Two, steps 1 and 2, page 29. From the piece you cut out of the frame, you will be creating two doors. To give clearance for the doors, cut a sliver off one long edge and one short edge, approximately $1/16$ inch (.15 cm). Cut the piece in half vertically to make the two doors. Cover the frame and both doors with paper and paint them. Hinge each door to the frame as you did the door in Shrine Two. (See photos 2-4.)

7 To keep the doors from swinging to the inside of the shrine, attach a doorstop to the inside of the frame opening. To make this doorstop, cut a narrow piece of foam board [about $1/2$ inch (1.3 cm) wide and slightly longer than the door opening]. Cover with paper on the front and top edge (the back won't show). Paint the doorstop the same color as the frame so it's unobtrusive.

8 From the back of the frame, glue this narrow piece to the bottom of the door opening, so just a narrow lip sticks above the frame opening. Now you can glue the frame to the shrine. Use embellishments to serve as doorknobs. (See photo 5.)

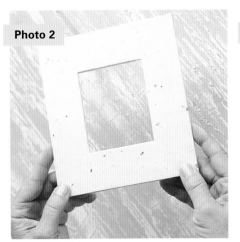
Photo 2

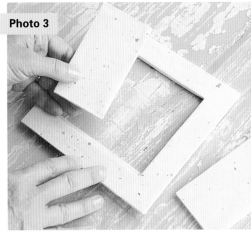
Photo 3

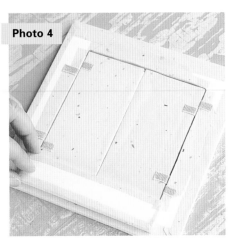
Photo 4

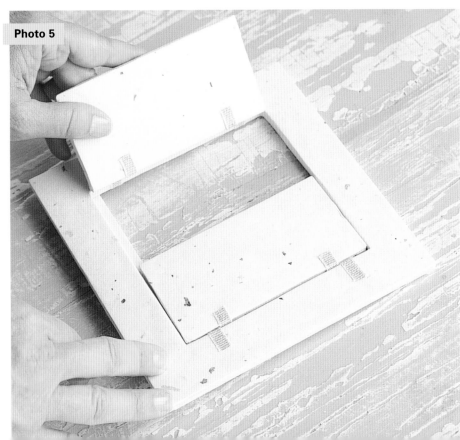
Photo 5

Shrine Seven

Tools

Utility knife

Cutting mat

Ruler

Pencil

Paper clips or bookmaker's
bone folder (optional)

Straight pins or string

Materials

Matte medium

Foam board [2 boards, approximately 22 x 28 inches
(56 x 71 cm), are sufficient]

White or cream-colored rice
paper (2 sheets), approximately
23 x 35 inches (58 x 89 cm).
(Note: Rice paper comes in many
different sizes. If you have paper
you want to use in other sizes,
you can adjust the amounts you
need accordingly. You will be cutting the sheets of paper, and
some of the pieces you will cut
out are small. It's possible, then,
that you can use several small
sheets of paper rather than the 2
larger ones directed here.)

Paper glue and
embellishment glue

Acrylic paints

Linen tape or narrow ribbon,
approximately 4 inches (10 cm)
long and $\frac{1}{4}$ inch (.6 cm) wide

Strong decorative paper,
approximately $9\frac{1}{2}$ (23 cm)
x 2 inches (5cm)

Collage and embellishment
materials

Shrine Seven

*Shrine Seven has interior niches,
and two drawers in the base.*

Instructions

1 Construct this shrine according
to the directions for Shrine
Three, page 33 (the door has a window in it and attaches like the door
in that shrine).

2 Note that a shelf runs horizontal-
ly across the inside of this shrine
with three niches underneath the
shelf (page 50.) I've given you the
dimensions for the niches pictured in
Shrine Seven, but you can make as
many or as few as you like, as large
or as small as you wish.

3 For the shelf, cut a piece of foam
board wide enough to go from
side to side on the inside of the
shrine, and the depth of the shrine.
Cover with paper.

4 Mark where you want this shelf
to go, and glue it into place.

5 Cut the upright pieces to make
the niches fit the height and
depth under the shelf.

DIMENSIONS

The finished size
of Shrine Seven is
12 inches high x 10 inches wide
x 4 inches deep
(30 x 25.5 x 10 cm).

The dimensions
of the foam board pieces are as follows:
Back wall, 12 x 10 inches (30 x 25.5 cm)
Ceiling, 10 x 2 inches (25.5 x 5 cm)
Side walls (2), $9\frac{1}{2}$ x 2 inches (24 x 5 cm)
Floor, $9\frac{1}{2}$ x 2 inches (24 x 5 cm)
Door, $9\frac{3}{4}$ x $9\frac{1}{2}$ inches (24.5 x 24 cm)
Interior shelf, $9\frac{1}{2}$ x 2 inches (24 x 5 cm)
Side walls for the niches (2),
2 x $2\frac{1}{2}$ inches each (5 x 6.5 cm)
Top and bottom pieces for the base,
$10\frac{1}{2}$ x 4 inches (27 x 10 cm) each
Back wall of the base,
$10\frac{1}{2}$ x $1\frac{1}{2}$ inches (27 x 4 cm)
Side walls of the base (2),
4 x $1\frac{1}{2}$ inches (10 x 4 cm)
Interior wall in base,
$2\frac{1}{4}$ x $1\frac{1}{2}$ inches (6 x 4 cm)
Inner false back of base,
$10\frac{1}{2}$ x $1\frac{1}{2}$ inches (27 x 4 cm)
Bottom of drawer (2),
$4\frac{1}{4}$ x 2 inches (10.5 x 5 cm)
Front of drawer (2), $4\frac{3}{4}$ inches
(12 cm) x less than 2 inches (5 cm)
Side walls of drawer (4),
2 x $1\frac{1}{4}$ inches (13 x 3 cm)
Back of each drawer, less than
5 inches x $1\frac{1}{4}$ inches (cut two)

Interior of Shrine Seven

6 Mark where you want them to go and glue them between the shelf and the floor. (See photo 1.)

7 Paint the shrine and collage and embellish as you wish.

8 Attach the roof.

9 To make the base with two drawers, start by constructing the base as you did in Shrine Three, step 9, page 34. (See Note preceding this step, as well.)

10 Measure the halfway point of the inside of the base, and glue in the interior wall which serves as the divider between the two drawers (remember to cover the cut piece of foam board first).

11 Glue in the inner back wall.

Photo 1

12 Now you're ready to construct the two drawers. The construction of a drawer is covered in Shrine 3, steps 10-15, pages 34-35.

I think you can see how I use the same basic techniques for constructing each of these shrines. I make larger, more complex structures by putting together various arrangements of doors, niches, and drawers. When you get the knack for making the more basic shrine, you'll be able to mix and match elements as well.

I've given you measurements to help you get started, but they are ultimately just suggestions. You can make the shrines any size you wish, in any proportion. Just decide what size you want the finished shrine to be and work it out from there. Once you cut the rectangle for the back, everything else follows the dimensions of that piece.

Be patient. If you work through the process, I think you will find it interesting and rewarding. And because it's so important, I'll repeat what I said earlier: Find what works for you. You may discover a better way, and if you do, please let me know!

Decorating Your Shrine

Now for the fun part. You've created a structure that is ready to be filled and decorated according to your own interests and artistic vision. The result will be a piece that is uniquely your own. To help you do that, I'm going to tell you exactly how I decorate my work, but I'm going to encourage you to use that information only as a springboard. Then, in the next section, A Maker's Dozen, 12 contemporary shrine artists show how they make their work distinctive and evocative.

Once I've built the shrine and painted it, I collage and embellish the inside. For me, the interior of the shrine contains the soul of the piece, the essence of the story I want to tell. I work on this part, adding and taking away elements, until I am satisfied. As you can imagine, and as the directions for construction noted, it is easier to work on the inside of the shrine before you attach the frame or doors.

A Collage Education

My shrines are dense with collage, like overlapping layers of memory. I don't plan them out in great detail, but instead gather up whatever ephemera (see pages 14-18 for a more detailed explanation) interests me. I may choose a map, an old letter, a ledger sheet or something else. As I mentioned earlier, I photocopy old paper items whenever it's possible so I can tear them as I wish. That is what I do next: tear the papers into shapes that will fit inside the shrine and then layer them in graduated sizes.

Sometimes I make transparencies of images, text, or photos by placing a piece of acetate in the copy machine instead of copy paper. I like to place a transparent photo over a map, or a poem over a photo. It adds to the mystery and invites the viewer in for a closer look. (When attaching a transparency, use the paper glue sparingly around the edges. It will dry clear so that you won't be able to see it.)

When I have an arrangement that pleases me, I glue it down with paper glue. This becomes the background for a vintage photo. I only use photocopies of these old photographs because I want to preserve the originals. Copy paper is thinner than actual photos, so it blends more easily into the background. I also tear around the image rather than use scissors to cut it out. This gives it a soft edge that also helps it blend into the background.

A Hint of Tint

After I have glued everything down, I go over the whole collage with a very light wash of acrylic paint, using the same color as that which I have used on the shrine and blotting with tissues as I go. The idea is to tint the collage, not cover it with the paint. You may want to experiment on some scraps of paper that you don't intend to use until you get the right mixture for the wash and master the technique of blotting. This wash of paint helps to unify everything, and also adds a mysterious air. Someone once remarked that the walls of my shrines contained the memories of the people who'd lived there. I almost kissed them because that was exactly the effect I was trying to achieve.

Once the wash is dry, I edge the photo and all the paper elements with a line of burnt umber acrylic paint (blotting and smudging as I go to again create that soft edge). Or sometimes I'll use a gold metallic pen, or a scribble of metallic oil pastels around the edges.

Embellishment Audition

As a final step, I add some embellishments, perhaps a few buttons or a key, or any of the dozens of items that I have collected and that crowd my studio shelves. I keep moving items around—auditioning them—until I come up with a pleasing arrangement. Often there are multiple possibilities and the choice is difficult. I look at how shapes work together. Do they intrigue the eye? How do they contribute to the story I have in mind? Sometimes I have to let the piece rest for a while. Then when I come back to it, I bring a fresh perspective.

I use a strong glue, as discussed in the Getting Started chapter (page 14), to make sure my embellishments stay where I place them. You will learn about some other techniques for attaching objects to your work in A Maker's Dozen.

Are We There, Yet?

I'm often asked how I know when a piece is finished. My shrines grow organically and at their own pace: sometimes painfully slowly, sometimes with sudden spurts as a child might. I have to pay close attention to how it's developing, and if I do, the shrine will "tell me" when it's done. Of course, sometimes I'm not listening and I go too far. The danger is having a preconceived idea of what the shrine should look like and trying to impose that idea on it instead of letting it become what it wants to be. The work is always better and richer, and has more soul, if I follow where it wants to lead me.

But what do I mean when I say the shrine will "tell me" when it's done? Practically speaking, I stand back and look at what I've done. If nothing nags at me, hinting that something just isn't right, or if I don't get the feeling that some area is missing something, then I know the shrine is

finished. On a more mysterious level, my pieces "sparkle" at me when they're complete. I see a tiny flash of light. Another artist I know told his class that when his piece has reached completion, he hears a tiny click, like the last piece of a jigsaw puzzle fitting into place. You may not see a sparkle or hear a click, but I am certain that if you are sensitive to your piece, it will tell you when it's done.

A Maker's Dozen

Over the years I have discovered a community of fellow artists who find the medium of shrines to be an ideal outlet for their creativity. Some of us work in shrines as our primary medium. Others may be creators of dolls, altered books, or even jewelry who decide to create a piece in their vernacular with the distinctive shrine-like qualities of enclosure and commemoration. We have met at art fairs and in workshops. We have encountered one another's work in galleries and publications and have sought each other out—sometimes to ask a question about technique or materials, or simply to say, "Your work has touched me."

This community of shrine makers has proven generous—eager to share and teach, as well as to create. I have learned much in conversations with other artists as we have discussed why and how we have come to our creations. In that spirit this next section, A Maker's Dozen, reveals the impetus and techniques behind the work of 12 contemporary shrine makers. From each artist, you will discover specific tips to assist you in your work and more ideas to inspire you. In their statements, and in those of the artists in the Gallery that follows, they talk about their work in their own words, giving you a sense of what it's like to share the ongoing conversation in our community.

Feeding a Fever

Sometimes when you have a story to tell, it seems as if things just arrive on their own and at the right time to make the piece come together.

Melissa Manley-Daniels
The Rose O'Neale Greenhow Papers, 2002
11½ x 14 x 3½ inches
(29 x 36 x 9 cm)
Cigar box, foam board, paper, steel wire, Spanish moss, dried roses, acrylic paint, ink, taffeta, glass beads, wood.

Process

1. This piece was made after Melissa Manley-Daniels, the artist, did research on a Confederate spy who was a heroine. The structure began with a wooden cigar box as the internal section.

2. On pieces made from a cigar box, the artist usually creates a foam board outer box to surround the smaller inner one, then adheres them with linen tape and glue.

3. Next, the whole piece is covered in a thin layer of papier mache to make it sturdier and to integrate the hybrid pieces.

4. If there are to be architectural elements such as columns, the artist likes to use modeling material and mat board to model them.

5. Whatever imagery has been chosen, such as letters or temple rubbings, is photocopied and then the copies are tinted with thinned acrylic paint or coffee to achieve the desired color.

Melissa Manley-Daniels

ARTIST STATEMENT:

Since childhood I've had a fascination with miniatures, dioramas in museums, and toy theaters. My language is that of graphic imagery, color, pattern, and layers. I often manifest my passion for a story or character by creating a miniature visual experience. The beauty of the box format is that it mimics a room or a shrine, elevating the subject matter to that of something removed from everyday life. The viewer's interest can be funneled to the inner sanctum. As opposed to a canvas, the shrine becomes interactive. The doors become parentheses around the subject. With my vignettes, I hope to portray small, frozen tableaux that convey some of the wonder or poignancy I originally felt about the subject.

If I am able to draw a viewer in and momentarily transport him or her to another magical place, then I am successful.

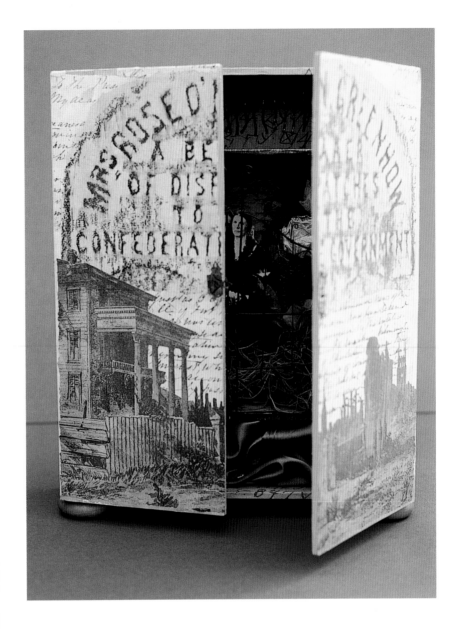

6. After they are dried, Melissa tears these colored paper images and glues them on the surface of the box using acrylic matte medium or an archival PVA glue.

7. Found-objects that fit the theme are attached by a variety of means including sewing, wiring, riveting, nailing or gluing.

8. The artist, a metalsmith, has discovered that wirework or metal accents are excellent additions to her work.

9. Hobby and hardware stores are a frequent source of new products, and Melissa likes to experiment to see how they'll work to achieve an effect.

Prismatic Scrims

An opaque or transparent sheet of fabric used as a theatrical backdrop, a scrim adds an element of drama to any creation.

Judy Hubbard
*Linked by Cora/Lena
Connections* Series, 1990
24 x 18 x 2¼ inches
(60 x 46 x 5.5 cm)
Silk tulle, color pencils,
photocopy, paint

Process

1. This layered fiber assemblage by Judy Hubbard was created using a direct-photocopy process. After ironing silk organza onto freezer paper, the artist fed the silk into a copy machine. Once the image was transferred, she stabilized it with a spray fixative and then carefully removed it from the freezer paper.

2. The printed silk was then ironed onto a heat-bonding material.

3. Individual design elements were cut out and ironed onto dyed silk chiffon or tulle that had been stretched taut over frames made from wood lathe.

4. Textile paints and color pencils were used to enhance the color of the images.

5. Each assemblage was comprised of a stack of three to five of these scrims, allowing fragments and images to "float" on several levels yet be viewed as a cohesive whole.

Judy Hubbard

ARTIST STATEMENT:

My series, *Lena Connections*, combines narrative and visual reflections on the life of my great aunt, Lena Buckner Tuten (1880-1905), the only other visual artist in my family. Each shrine explores the enduring nature of artistic work and the ability of creative energy to bridge time. Although I did not begin with the idea of building shrines, the end result of these complex, layered-silk constructions is a reverential honoring of my relationship with Lena, who I never knew.

White on White

The layers of texture and riot of colors that characterize most shrines made from found objects can be provocative, but in this monochromatic work, the dominance of a single shade works a subtle spell.

Judi Riesch
Kindred Soul, 2003
8½ x 5½ x 3½ inches
(21 x 14 x 9 cm)
Wood curio cabinet, acrylic paints, gel medium, vintage photograph and papers, trims, buttons, feathers, bisque dolls, twine, ivory pieces, shells, and wax

Judi Riesch

Process

1. The small curio cabinet was one the artist, Judi Riesch, had on a table in her family room for several years. It housed a series of found objects, always changing according to whim.

2. She had just finished working in a collaborative color journal project and had become intrigued with working with nothing but whites. This small white cabinet seemed perfect for exploring the idea.

3. Using paints and wax, she distressed the wood and chose the inside pages of a vintage photo album as the base. The vintage photograph of these kindred young spirits was placed within the album opening to create depth.

4. The theme of "two" is repeated throughout, using the bisque doll figures embedded in wax and twine, as well as in the feathers.

5. The vintage trim and pieces of doilies frame the work, giving it a theater feeling.

6. As a result of the limited palette, the subtlety of the white-on-white textures revealed themselves.

ARTIST STATEMENT:

I have always loved paper and vintage objects for as long as I can remember. Working primarily with found objects that I have collected over the years, I find a challenge in creating a new life for these discarded fragments. Using paints, papers, and wax as layering elements, I construct shadow boxes, cabinets, or artist books with these objects. Each vintage treasure that I am drawn to seems to have a story to tell, and I see myself as the storyteller.

A Book Is a Box

It's not just that the shape is right, or that the pages are easily carved to make niches: a book also lends its words and history to the aura of your shrine.

Beth Cote
Bessie, 2002
17 x 8 x 5 inches (43 x 20 x 12.5 cm)
Silk chiffon, water-slide decal paper with old photo copied, bobbin, starfish, buttons and other found objects, pigment ink

Beth Cote

Process

1. This shrine by Beth Cote began with an old book of sheet music, opened to a page the artist wanted to use as the backdrop. She glued the book open by rubbing matte gel medium into the edges of the book with her finger (you could use a small paintbrush), then leaving it open to dry.

2. She cut three shallow holes through the pages to fit the items she wanted to showcase. She drew the hole in the size needed with a pencil and then used a craft knife to cut into the book. The depth of each hole was determined by setting the object into it, then cutting deeper if necessary.

3. Pigment ink was applied directly onto the book pages starting with the lightest color and working to the darkest, then adding a burnt copper accent to the edges.

4. Three-dimensional items were glued into the niches with gel and allowed to dry.

5. The artist color copied an old photo to water-slide decal according to the directions, then ironed this transfer to silk chiffon per the directions on package.

6. The chiffon was then cut to size to fit around the book. Using pins, the pieces of chiffon were brought together with the book inside. Then, using a sewing machine, Beth sewed around the edges so they were rough. To get the desired effect, she ripped a hole in the chiffon and burned the edges of it.

ARTIST STATEMENT: Books have shaped me. As a child, I would absorb the words and be forever changed. As an adult, the perfect vessel for my art is a book. It represents the body of my subconscious and the world I live in. It is ever-changing, as is my mind and the meaning of my art, and it can be translated in many ways. This book is dedicated to my great grandmother, who I never met but feel as if I knew from the wonderful stories that my grandmother shared about her. The found objects in the niches are a reflection of her.

Dorrit Title
Dinner with Great Grandmother, 2001
17 x 13½ x 5 inches
(44 x 34.5 x 13 cm)
Old wooden desk drawer, cyanotype print made from old photo, silverware, dried rose, liqueur glass, door lock, key, candles, small tray, doily, wallpaper, copy of letter, watercolor wash

Smallness Equals Intimacy

The diminutive wooden drawer that houses this shrine requires the viewer to focus attention directly on the piece, and in the process, creates a deep connection.

Dorrit Title

Process

1. The small desk drawer that artist Dorrit Title used for this piece gives a sense of intimacy to the objects that surround the picture.

2. A photo of the artist's Great Grandmother Fanny Gahlberg as a young woman in Vienna, was made into a negative and then printed as a cyanotype to give it the blue color. (Cyanotype is an antique photo process.)

3. The silverware was attached with small nails and craft glue was used for the other objects.

4. The wallpaper is self-adhesive.

ARTIST STATEMENT: I work in a variety of media including collage, painting, and printmaking. The shrines I have created are a tribute to the memory of my maternal great grandmother and grandparents who died in the Holocaust. I have used this art form to bring to life the strength of their souls, and the beauty of spirit.

Through a Glass Deeply

Some shrines are covered in glass to protect the objects inside, others may use pieces of glass as statements, but Madonna Phillips creates images on the glass itself to add an additional layer of meaning to her work.

Madonna Phillips
Protective Coating,
2002
30 x 40 x 3 inches
(76 x 102 x 7.5 cm)
Wood, glass, mirror,
found objects

Process

1. Both found and constructed boxes are used to house the objects in this artist's shrines.

2. Flea markets, estate sales, thrift shops, family albums and yearbooks are just some of the sources that provide what the artist calls "the detritus of memory that I use in my work."

3. Shoes, spools, threads, letters, beads and keys, photos, clothes, old magazines, buttons—these provide "what is lost but can be found for art."

4. Glass and mirror are surfaces to be painted on and attached to the boxes filled with objects.

5. Extra heavy acrylic gel is a good adhesive for attaching mirrors or glass, as is jeweler's glue.

6. Dental glue also works well for some glass problems.

Madonna Phillips

ARTIST STATEMENT: My work is based on the experience of growing up in mid-century America. My process is much like that of the Southern writer: exploring what I know, then drawing a visual narrative that presents part of the story, the rest to be completed by the viewer. After working for many years in a stained glass studio, drawing the traditional cartoons and painting on the surface of glass, I am now using some of those skills to do collage and oil on mirror glass. I like the reflective qualities—it's a good material for my Proustian journey. I endeavor to taste the memory, to receive a glint of the experiences of other human beings, and to blend it with my own.

Habitat for Energy

A shrine is more than a collection of objects. In the way the elements interact with one another they create an energy that is greater than the sum of the parts.

Nancy Hoerner
Noreen's Blue Habitat, 2001
22 x 7 x 7 inches (56 x 18 x 18 cm)
Wood, collage, embelllishment

Nancy Hoerner

Process

1. Each of Nancy Hoerner's habitats is constructed from cigar and other wooden boxes.

2. Wooden beads, candleholders, or drawer pulls are added as feet. Each has a finial, monogram, address, mailbox, and key. The addresses are made from objects with numbers ranging from computer keys to screen window numbers.

3. The outsides are collaged with magazine and newspaper pictures of buildings, trees, and landscapes. The insides are collaged using pictures of curtained windows and Persian rugs.

4. When the collage is complete, a wash of acrylic paint is added.

5. Architectural items such as door plates, keyhole plates, hinges, drawer pulls, drawer knobs, thermometers, and wooden gingerbread pieces (some made for dollhouses) are glued to the surface.

6. There is always a small circuit board for energy.

ARTIST STATEMENT: I decided I could not define my alter ego, Noreen Howard, well enough to make a doll, but I wanted an outlet for the creativity that was coming from her. Noreen loved collecting things and also collecting other people's collections. I needed someplace to put all this wonderful stuff. That was when the habitat idea came to me. I have three habitats (shrines) to date and have a fourth one in progress.

Hope and Healing

Heidi Darr-Hope's work demonstrates that creating a shrine can have therapeutic benefit for those who are chronically or terminally ill, and for their loved ones, as well.

Heidi Darr-Hope
In Adoration, 2002
25 x 40 x 8 inches (63 x 102 x 20 cm)
Mixed media

Process

1. Finding the objects is the first step in creating a reliquary for healing. Heidi Darr-Hope believes we are intuitively drawn to certain objects and images in our environment because of their symbolic reference. As the shrine maker collects objects relating to the theme she has decided on, the objects that appear may begin to change that theme. It is important to be sensitive to changing thoughts in this time and remember that this is a process, the artist says.

2. A box may be found or constructed specifically for the shrine. Colors are chosen to reflect the mood the artist wants to create. The enclosure may be painted or collaged. If collage is used, intentions, blessings or prayer can be written on the scraps of paper.

3. The help of others can be used any time it feels appropriate to the person creating the shrine.

4. A shape is chosen for the symbolic center of the shrine (square, rectangle, oval, triangle, circle) and cut from sturdy material—thin balsa wood or Luan works well. It should be large enough to fill the top half of the structure. Two holes are drilled equidistant in the top of the shape to be used later to suspend it from the ceiling.

5. A symbol should be painted or a symbolic object glued to the center of this shape. A painted eye could remind the maker and viewers to look inward; an object from nature might suggest the healing power of the earth; a small glass bottle could contain elements collected from a sacred place.

6. Paint bands of color, glue beads or found objects around the symbol, creating a safe nest for it.

7. Use a cup hook or a screw and copper wire to suspend the shape from the center of the ceiling.

8. Decorate the shrine with prayer ribbons—like small Tibetan prayer flags. The artist suggests at least 20 strips of ribbon cut as long as the shrine. Small charms, beads, or amulets can be tied to the bottom of each ribbon, and with each knot, the maker can say a prayer or think of an intention. Cup hooks, upholstery tacks, or screw eyes can be used in the ceiling as devices for tying on the prayer ribbons.

9. Select objects to be placed in your shrine. You may want to change the objects over time—to reflect the changing seasons or the rhythms of your life—so don't attach them. You may also want to write prayers or intentions on beautiful paper fragments, folding them thoughtfully and tucking them into the reliquary. Friends, family, caregivers, and your healers can be encouraged to add to this part of the process, if you wish.

10. Use your reliquary as a focus for meditation, prayer, or reflection. Set a time to dust and clean it at least once a year, not allowing it to become static, but keeping it as a living, changing, growing work of life.

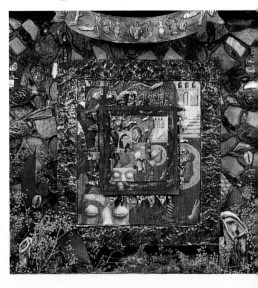

ARTIST STATEMENT: *The Reliquaries of Healing* are a series that began from my need to express and honor the sacred. Many cultural and spiritual traditions are embodied within these works as I continuously draw upon worldwide theological concerns to enrich and deepen my search for truth. As an artist in residence at a cancer hospital in Columbia, South Carolina, I have created what I call an "interactive healing reliquary" where patients, family members, staff, and community visitors are invited to write their thoughts, blessings, and prayers on slips of paper and place them in this shrine. Several hundred are received every month. I believe found objects are a way to give emotions voice. Taking pieces of earth and sky and incorporating them with other objects allows intuition to guide you to an icon.

Turn the Page

Mounted so it can be hung for contemplation, this shrine fashioned from a book can also be taken down so you can look through it for a closer read of its meaning.

Karen Michel
Little Altar Book, 2003
9 x 11 x 3 inches (23 x 28 x 7.5 cm)
Mixed media book

Process

1. This shrine in a book was inspired by the tin work and little altars or nichos of Mexico. Karen Michel envisioned having a book that she could turn to for inspiration, holding personal archetypes within the pages while also paying homage to them.

2. The piece is mounted on board and wired so it works as a wall piece.

3. The metalwork on the board was achieved with aluminum ventilation tape that was etched with a stylus, then a patina was added with India ink.

4. The book itself is hand-bound with an old, recycled book cover.

5. A wood frame was added to the cover to give a recessed view of the hand-carved heart stamp and to also support the nail that holds the book shut (along with the key string).

6. All of the pages and the cover were first prepared with gesso to prime and strengthen them.

7. The main ingredients for the majority of the pages are watercolor pigment crayons layered and sealed with acrylic-gel medium. The various processes explored are inkjet image transfers, hand-carved stamps, collage, and drawing.

Karen Michel

ARTIST STATEMENT: My passion for creating is an innate response to my relation to my environment and the search for truth that follows. Experiencing and portraying the spiritual and the physical, these images are intended to emanate a feeling of mindfulness—both of ourselves and of our surroundings. Visual prayers, mantras—they are reminders to keep searching for the beauty and discovering the abundance that is within our environment and ourselves.

It Starts With a Photo

Sometimes the found photo of someone you've never known speaks to you as intimately as if you were its subject's best friend. Here is a way to reply.

Lynne Perrella
Young Will, 2002
7½ x 11½ x 4½ inches (18 x 28 x 11 cm)
Photo, cigar box, ephemera, found objects, paint and varnish

Lynne Perrella

Process

1. Lynne Perrella found a compelling vintage photo of a boy with the words "Young Will" written in pencil on the back. She thought poor Will looked beleaguered, as if he carried the weight of the world on his slim shoulders; his eyes haunted. As soon as she "met" Will she wanted to continue his story in her artwork.

2. The box was made, quite experimentally, by taking a somewhat new and uninteresting cigar box and gluing an inexpensive picture frame to the front. The artist enjoys the challenge of appropriating odd bits and pieces to create her own version of a traditional shadow box.

3. The box/frame was covered with antique seed catalog pages.

4. The rusted antique "medallion" at the top of the piece was discovered at a metal salvage lot. It works because it is old, worn to a beautiful patina, and it looks flower-like.

5. Fabric flowers splattered with acrylic paints sit on the top of an old piece of wooden type. Bent nails encrusted with wax are glued in place.

6. Lynne wanted the viewer to have to navigate lots of veils and layers to actually discover Will, so peering inside the box you see splatters of black India ink, old chicken wire, unraveled loops of natural twine, and the photo of Will.

7. Hardware store golden varnish provides the finishing touches.

ARTIST STATEMENT: Will looks very much at home in this piece, which comes as a relief to me. I have often wondered what his story was and how his life ended up. Old photos of unknown souls are a real entry point to creativity, although I also like the intimacy of using my own family photos for my work. Either way it's an opportunity to make up tales, writing happy endings for all the stories.

Journal of the Journey

Thoughts and images gathered over time have a way of rearranging themselves to suggest a theme that needs exploring.

Janice Lowry
Resting, 2000
20 x 14 x 4½ inches
(51 x 36 x 11 cm)
Mixed media,
found objects

Process

1. Journals are Janice Lowry's source of inspiration. She has been keeping them for 30 years, putting drawings, thoughts, newspaper articles, and collages in them. Recently she has been documenting from newspaper articles how faces are covered (e.g. surgical masks, reality game equipment, religious dress).

2. After building up visual and word resources in the journals, she begins making boxes, usually using soft wood such as pine. The tools are simple: jigsaw, sander, and drill.

3. The objects are placed in boxes, and they sit on the floor for approximately a week to a month. As the artist passes by, she adds and takes away objects.

4. Once Janice is satisfied with the content of the boxes, she attaches each piece in a permanent way. She usually screws the objects to the wood, which means she has to work from the back of the box, moving forward.

5. Hanging the shrine-in-progress allows for an additional look, and the chance to rearrange before the glass is added. The artist says her work is 80 percent redoing the art.

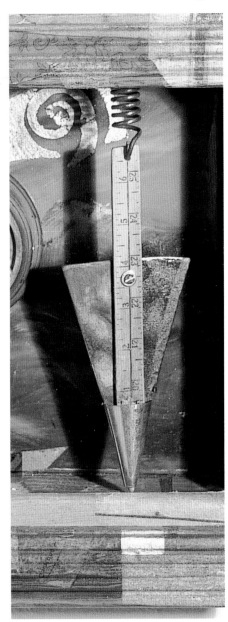

ARTIST STATEMENT: I first started assemblage work and creating shrines when I was a fine arts major in college. I went to thrift stores looking for old frames to cut up to fit my paintings. Then I used the leftover pieces in the art. The shapes of the art were a reference to houses and my experiences as a Catholic looking at shrines in churches. My influences have been Joseph Cornell, Dadaism, surrealisim and folk art. My materials are found in many locations. When we travel I go to flea markets and antique stores. I alter the objects in such a way as to have my touch on them. My goal is that when the objects are placed in the box, they become transformed.

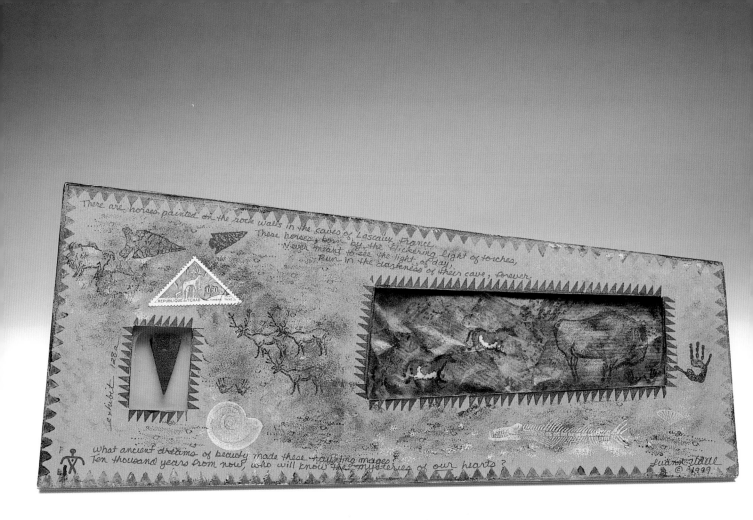

Continuing the Journey

In many cultures, shrines are placed along the path of a pilgrimage so seekers can stop for contemplation. Luann Udell's mail-art shrines make the journey themselves, provoking those who see them along the way to ponder their mysteries.

Luann Udell
I Dream of Horses: Horse Artifacts, 1999
7 x 17 x ¾ inches (18 x 43 x 2 cm)
Foam board, mat board, assorted papers, cloth tape, postage stamps, acrylic paint, sea glass, polymer clay, and shells

Process

1. The journey this piece takes is part of the creation. Just like a regular postcard, the giant mail postcard touches every one who gets to see it, including the mail carrier. Luann Udell makes a point of walking a new mailing to the post office, showing it off to everyone along the way.

2. Two pieces of mat board make a postcard "sandwich" that can have windows and niches. Check with the post office to make sure what dimensions will meet postal regulations.

3. The windowed niche should be small [2 x 3 inches (5 x 7.5 cm) is a good, stable size with room for viewing], allowing at least ½ inch (1.25 cm) of space from the edges of the card.

4. Underneath the window opening is a clear piece of acetate (a section cut from a report cover, available at an office supply store, is perfect). Tape the acetate on the inside of the mat board.

5. The objects for the shrine in the niche can be anchored for the journey with glue or not, allowing them to rearrange themselves on the trip.

6. The outside edges of the card are sealed with wide, colored tape to protect them. (And it looks cool, too!) Colored or black masking tape, bookbinding tape, cloth tape, even hockey stick wrapping tape (inexpensive and it comes in several colors) can be used.

7. The outer surface is then decorated by stamping, covering with collage or paint, and/or gluing items or drawing on the surface. The more thoroughly the raw edges and construction marks are covered, the more mysterious the piece becomes.

8. The card may be addressed to the artist or to a friend in a decorative, but also easily legible, fashion.

9. To add a special touch to the work, Luann visits the post office or stamp store and finds stamps with images or themes to complement the work.

Luann Udell

ARTIST STATEMENT: My work is inspired by the Lascaux cave paintings in southern France. These paintings of ancient animals—horses, bison, bulls, and red deer—are reinterpreted in my artwork. Everything from my life in the past finds a new place in my present work. From my studies in art history and archaeology come the themes that enrich my art: preservation of artifacts, restoration of their content, interpretation of their meaning. I moved from traditional quilting to using fabric as a collage statement. I combine antique, vintage and new fibers with my own polymer clay artifacts, carved and polished to resemble real prehistoric items. I want to evoke the sense of real artifacts from lost cultures. And storytelling—I believe it is the stories in my work that forge the strong connections with my audience. They are stories about the power of those cave paintings, their fragility in modern times, and the enduring qualities of the human heart.

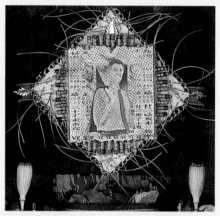

Gallery

The 19 artists whose work appears in this gallery share a common intention: the creation of artistic shrines. But as you have seen—and will continue to discover, the expression of this intention can take many forms. A shrine may look like a figure, be worn as jewelry, hang on the wall or sit on a table top. Its message may be slyly humorous, reverential, mystical or deliberately obscure. Colors may be bold or muted, the style may be sleek or complex—or somewhere in between. The possibilities seem to be limitless.

In the statements accompanying their work, the artists share with you what sparked their imagination, and give you glimpses of how they brought their visions to life. It's my hope that these images and words will spark a creative fire in you, as well.

In these two pieces, I was trying to celebrate the ordinary and discarded object, both natural and manmade. These objects are things that I have found on walks over the years. I consider them sacred because of their simple and unusual beauty, as well as their gift of inspiration.

Akira Blount
Sacred Relics, 2002
32 x 6 x 4 inches (80 x 15 x 10 cm)

Akira Blount
Sacred Circles, 2002
33 x 6 x 4 inches (80 x 15 x 10 cm)
Cloth, found metal, leather, antique
fabric, twigs, grapevine tendrils, and
other found materials. The coloring on
the faces is done with colored pencil.

Janet Hofacker

ARTIST STATEMENT:

My passion for the creative process

is evident in my art.

Janet Hofacker
Beatrice, 2001
5 x 12 x 5 inches (13 x 30 x 12.5 cm)
Wood recycled box, acrylic paints, recycled picture frame, photo of Beatrice Wood, two candlestick holders, sequins, dimensional paints, rubber stamp "DADA", black pigment ink, flat glass marbles, glass ball, plastic altered letters, brass candlestick for stand

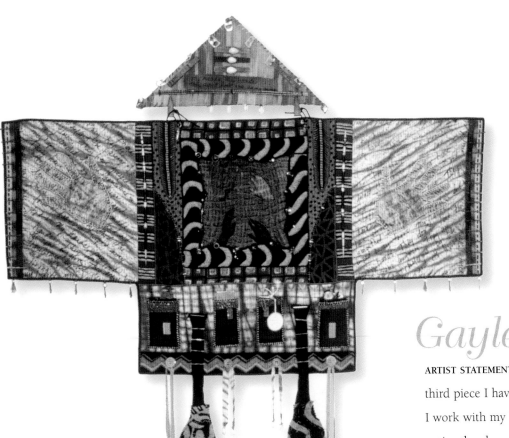

Gayle Pritchard
Celebration of (Mid) Life: My Hands
Don't Look the Same Anymore, 1997
45 x 30 x 2 inches (115 x 76 x 5 cm)
Photo transfer of original photograph, hand-dyed
cotton, silk organza, hand-printed fabric, metallic
thread, commercial fabrics, fabric paint, embroidery
floss, found objects, charms, beads, porcupine
spines, foam board, antique cotton, narrative

Gayle Pritchard

ARTIST STATEMENT: This shrine to my hands is the
third piece I have made about turning forty. Because
I work with my hands constantly, I can't help but
notice the changes. This piece celebrates my relationship with my hands and the beautiful objects
they help me to create. It also examines the genuine
surprise I feel each day when I look at my "new"
hands. It's as if I've just discovered them.

My journal entry of January 28, 1997 tells the story:
"My hands, my hands reflect the passage of time.
They have grasped and clenched, folded themselves
on my lap, stood on my hips. They have slapped
and hugged, stroked, caressed, and made love.
They have stitched and been stitched, smoothed the
folds of fabric, and wiped away the tears. My hands,
my hands. They don't look the same anymore.
They are transformed by life and its living."

Inga Hunter
Left to right,
Leopard Man, 1998
Legba, 1998
Africa, 1998
Erzulie, 1998
12 x 16 x 6 inches
(30 x 40 x 15 cm)
Mahoe wood from
Jamaica, mixed media

Inga Hunter

ARTIST STATEMENT: A Haitian friend once
came into our house and said, "But these
are all shrines. You have shrines and
altars everywhere." I had never really
seen my work in those terms, because I
had always done it unconsciously. I
think the work was a form of anchoring,
because I have always felt displaced. And
when I discovered my Jamaican family
with its West African origins, my world
was turned around. I started to study the
horror of the African Diaspora.

Caribbean people find it almost impossible to trace African backgrounds because no records were kept. I felt a need to express my past—to celebrate it, and to forgive my ancestors. So the whole series of shrines came to be. I decided that all I could do was to trust my intuition, to go where I responded most strongly. I made a series of Minkisi images. These are vessels with an outward spirit and visible signs of an inward and spiritual relationship with God. They are hiding places for people's souls, receptacles for sacred medicines given to mankind. Not just simple fetishes, they are highly complex means for healing and for honoring ancestors. I made one for all my female ancestors who had my name. I'm still making them.

My understanding of myself may have changed from one sort of displacement to another, but my working methods are still the same. I work in assemblage, bricolage, layers. I have always used fabric, paper, paint, blood, bones, glue, beads, feathers, what I find in the road—anything that seems to be right. My earlier work was in the form of artifacts from invented cultures of my own. This isn't so very different. It is just my own interpretation of my unknown past.

Keith Lo Bue

ARTIST STATEMENT: I began my journey as a maker with a compulsion to make enclosures: spaces that house mystery and wonder. Fifteen years later, although my material focus and technical palette are considerably different, secret spaces are still pouring out of me. Whether as physical objects or arrangements of pixels, the materials that thrill me continue to peek out from the homes I've fashioned for them. Their homes are, perhaps inevitably, mine.

Keith Lo Bue
Wrecked and Rescued , 2003
4½ x 3 x ¾ (10.25 x 7.5 x 1 cm)
Jeweler's wooden bench pin,
art deco cuff links, Masonic
ceremonial belt adornment,
porcelain bust, green glass,
steel wire, engravings, Victorian
silk and costume beads,
restoration glass, paper, text, soil

Keith Lo Bue
Angels Unawares, 2001
Pendant, closed:
3 x 2¼ x 1¼ inches
(7.5 x 5.25 x 1.25 cm)
Pendant, open:
3 x 4½ x 1¼ inches
(7.5 x 10.25 x 1.25 cm)
Modified Victorian
display case, glass,
iron wire, waxed linen
thread, brass hardware,
ambrotype, engravings,
opals, tin ornamental
studs, sea urchin
spines, Victorian ruby
glass, leather, paper,
text, soil

Sharon McCartney
Botany: Questions and Answers, 2003
6¾ x 4½ x ¾ inches (17 x 11 x 2 cm)
Old textbook, watercolor, acrylic, pastel, pencil,
gelatin prints, vintage papers, gesso, tea bag
paper, thread, dried lavender buds, seeds and
acorn caps

Sharon McCartney

ARTIST STATEMENT: My work commemorates personal experience and evinces specific memories. For me, art begins with my longtime habit of collecting natural objects on walks through land near my home. My subjects are ephemeral: wildflowers, birds, insects, animals, and plants from all seasons, found in the New England woods. I am inspired by daily contact with the natural world and by travel. My books are forums for play and experimentation as I combine organic forms with diverse textures, abstract or unconventional compositions, and eclectic patterning. My work is about my relationship to the natural world as a source of sanctuary, wonder, and personal rhythm.

Maria Consuelo Moya

ARTIST STATEMENT: My passion for shrines comes from the framework of the dreams, emotions, and magic encountered in my life. Focusing on the minute details of color, shape, and texture takes me on a journey of exploration. My challenge is to share that journey with the viewer and to arouse an emotional connection to the visual elements of everyday life. The objects have a spiritual quality all their own.

Maria Consuelo Moya
El Corazon, 2003
7½ x 3¾ x 4 inches
(19 x 9.5 x 10 cm)
Wood box, foam board, mat board, embossed/hand-stamped metal, embroidery, glass beads, ribbon, metal findings, yarn, found objects, sequins, metal beads, Indian paper, gold flecks, ribbon roses and Japanese mizuhiki

Maria Consuelo Moya
Mi Querido, David, 2003
8¼ x 6 x 2⅝ inches (21 x 6 x 7.25 cm)
Wood box, foam board, mat board, hand-tinted photo, tulle, metallic braid, poppy pods, waxed thread, ornamental fruit, metal findings, metallic ribbon, tissue, pipe cleaners, silk, brass, glass beads, bamboo, marble, and embossed paper

Maria Consuelo Moya
Memories of Friendship, 2003
7½ x 5¾ x 2¼ inches (19 x 15 x 6 cm)
Wood crate, foam board, mat board, handmade wooden shelf and boxes, woven straw mat, poppy pods, daylily stems, hens and chickens dried stems, horsehair, toothpicks, beads, tatting, wooden wheels (tiny), metal findings, embossed paper, metallic tissue paper, bone calaveras, ribbon, paper flowers, and glass beads

Karron Nottingham
Our Lady of the Highway, Pray for Us, 1996
16 x 8 x 9 inches (40 x 20 x 22.5 cm)
Wood, color copy, foam board, plaster, nails,
glitter, sequins, waxed linen, found objects

Karron Nottingham

ARTIST STATEMENT: My mixed media are a means of expressing satirical life plays on the essence of womanhood. They embrace the notion that we all have "stories to tell."

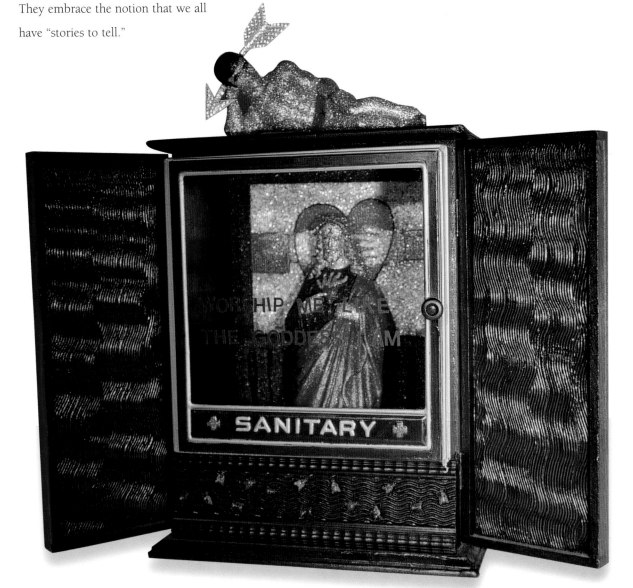

Karron Nottingham
Worship Me Like The Goddess I Am, 2001
24 x 20 x 10 inches (60.5 x 51 x 25.5 cm)
Found wooden box, biscuit box, molding, glass, statuary, glitter, nails, plastic flies, signage, acrylic paint, oil paint, acrylic resin, Christmas lights

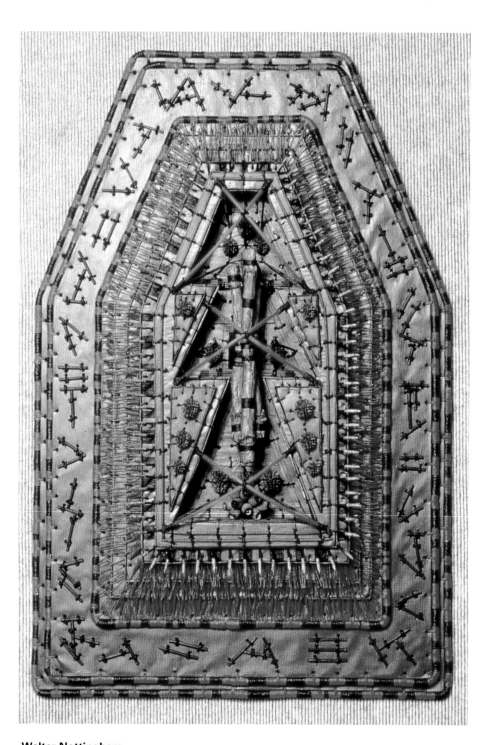

Walter Nottingham

ARTIST STATEMENT: The atmosphere that my work presents to the viewer is my main concern. Each of my works is an attempt to articulate the spiritual and aesthetic content of an object that is enshrined. The media I use to give these feelings and ideas "form" are mainly handmade paper, special objects (that I enshrine in packages), and natural fibers. My shrines are best related to religious folk art and crafts.

Walter Nottingham
Shrine 15, 2001
18 x 27 x 6 inches
(46 x 68.5 x 15 cm)
Mixed media

Walter Nottingham
Shrine 6, 2000
18 x 26 x 5 inches
(46 x 66 x 13 cm)
Mixed media

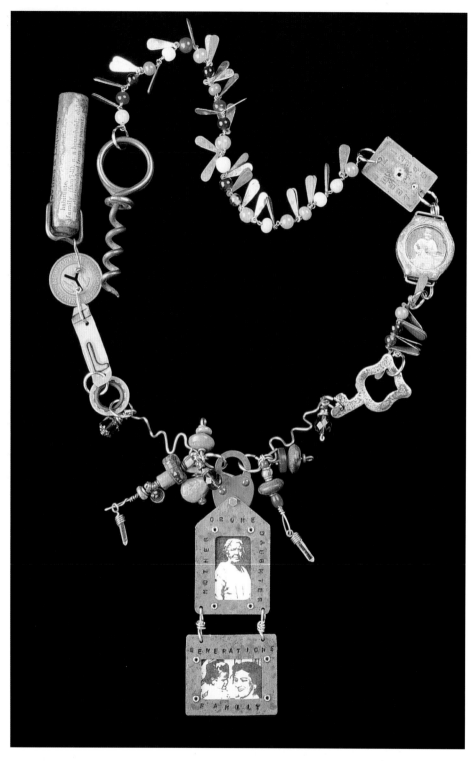

Linda O'Brien

ARTIST STATEMENT: Creating intimate spaces has always been a part of who I am. A small stone taken from my father's grave when I was five consoled me for many years. I put it in a special box with a photo and trinkets that had value only to me. I suppose that was my first shrine. As a self-taught artist, I create my pieces more from an intuitive feeling rather than a learned

Linda O'Brien
Daughter-Mother-Crone, 2003
Necklace, 24 inches (30 cm)
Mixed media, recycled materials

technique. This allows me the freedom to make and break my own rules. My work, although very eclectic, seems to be a continuing series of personal icons, altars and shrines honoring people, places, and archetypes to which I feel a connection. The fact that I do this using organic, recycled, and found materials just makes it all the better.

Linda O'Brien
Shrine to Life, 2003
Necklace, 20 inches (25 cm)
Mixed media, recycled materials

Opie O'Brien

ARTIST STATEMENT: My conceptual approach to creating art was first developed through music when I was very young. As with visual art, music is fundamentally a human emotional experience. I started formal instruction at an early age and it was based on structure, discipline and exactness—precepts now rooted in my brain. I was once told "music is mathematics." I've had many teachers throughout my life (and it has been a joyous journey) who have helped refine the subtle nuances and have redefined the aesthetics of musicianship. No matter what I'm working on, I try to let the structure and discipline be the backdrop of the piece. For me, the true success of a piece happens when it affects someone on a purely emotional level, for then it has touched the soul.

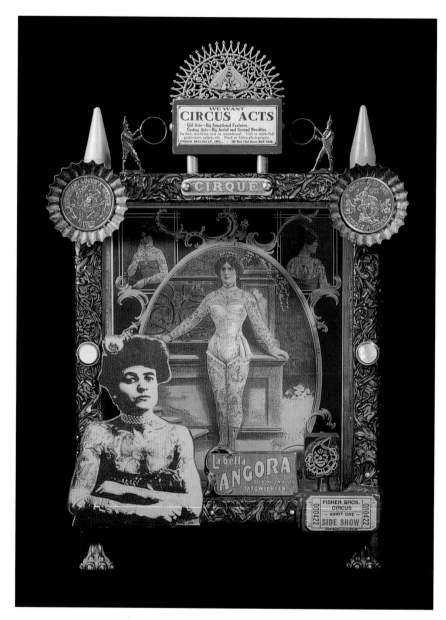

Opie O'Brien
La Bella Angora, 2002
17 x 10 x 3 inches (43 x 25 x 7.5 cm)
Mixed media and recycled materials

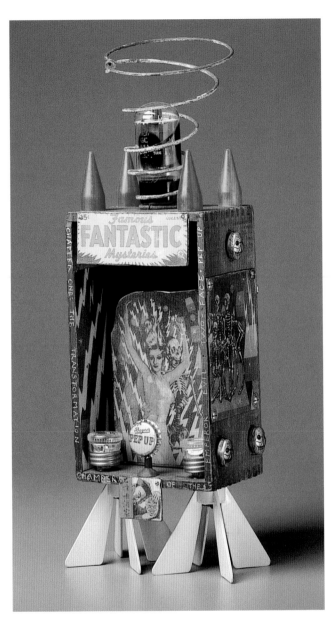

Opie O'Brien
The Transformation Chamber, 2002
14 x 5 x 4 inches (35 x 12.5 x 10 cm)
Mixed media and recycled materials

Opie O'Brien
Land of Enchantment, 2002
24 x 13½ x 7½ inches (60 x 34 x 19 cm)
Mixed media and recycled materials

Linda & Opie O'Brien

ARTISTS STATEMENTS: They say opposites attract, and for us that is so true on many levels. Opie is disciplined and detail oriented, his execution of a piece is flawless, and his methods of joinery are pure poetry. His original concept becomes his completed piece. My style is much looser, never fully planned in advance. I do eventually merge with my original concept but on a more abstract level than Opie does.

We were artists when we met. Opie is both an artist and a musician. He attended the School of Visual Arts in New York, and played Carnegie Hall at age 23 and Madison Square Garden at age 28. He was in the Raspberries, Tommy James & the Shondells, and played with some amazing musicians. I am completely self-taught and my style can only be described as raw and primitive. Yet it's because of our different approaches, that we believe we excel as a team.

Linda and Opie O'Brien
Prom Night: 1940, 2003
4 x 10 x 2½ inches (10 x 25.5 x 6.5 cm)
Mixed media and recycled materials

Linda and Opie O'Brien
The Portal of Chronos, 2002
2 ¾ x 7½ x 1½ inches (17 x 19 x 4 cm)
Mixed media and recycled materials

As a rule we work independently, but when we do collaborate, it involves a lot of brainstorming. Usually one of us will get a concept and then we bounce ideas back and forth until it feels right. When we work together, each of us contributes in our individual areas of expertise.

Prom Night is a shrine to Opie's parents' prom night. Even Lady Liberty (a 1940 silver half dollar) is dressed for the occasion. The two antique toy blocks represent their names, Marty and Marion. Underneath their image (on cloth) their high school rings are permanently

attached on each side of a watch face representing Time. *The Portal of Chronos* represents a metaphorical journey into our past, present, and future.

Gena Ollendieck

ARTIST STATEMENT: I am inspired by a combination of found objects, nature and 16th-century fine hand-bound books. The techniques of hand binding, leather work, and mixed media sculpture and assemblage allow my creations of suspended found objects encased in hand-bound book form to be used as an artist's or functional book. I use natural and found objects and dramatize them, striving for the feelings that coexist between the natural, physical, and imaginary worlds. Old machine parts, metal, older photographic images, stone, and found objects move, turn, and are suspended in the book cover, creating an unexpected relationship between form and function and imagination and reality.

Gena Ollendieck
Waste No Time, Dream Now, 2003
9½ x 6 x 4 inches (20 x 14 x 10 cm)
Paper, leather, found objects,
photographic images, wood, metal

Gena Ollendieck
Live Now…Yes You, 2003
28 x 13 x 6 inches (71 x 33 x 15 cm)
Paper, leather, found objects, metal, wood, stone,
wood type. (Hand- bound leather book within the
sculptural assemblage is functional; it can be
removed to be used as an album. The house
assemblage is a place for the album to live.)

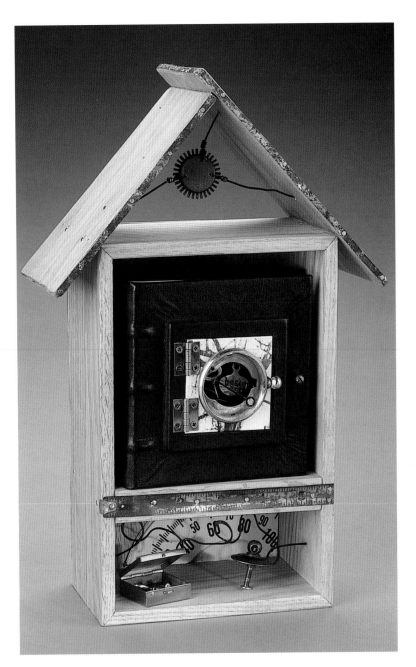

Gena Ollendieck
Key To It All, 2003
8 x 5½ x 4 inches (20 x 14 x 10 cm)
Paper, leather, found objects, photographic
images, wood, lead type, metal

Ira Ono
Tablets of Time, 2002
18 x 32 x 2 inches
(46 x 80 x 5 cm)
Mixed media

Ira Ono

ARTIST STATEMENT: I see a great beauty in objects discarded and altered by time.
I seek them out. For me, discovering a beach or an old abandoned house that can
be culled through is like dying and going to heaven! Many of the pieces in my work
include elements and discoveries found on Hawaii's beaches, reclaimed and made
sacred again. Many of the pieces contain my original Japanese paste paper.
My work is said to have an "altar-like" quality. At first look a piece might appear
to be quite bejeweled, but closer inspection reveals items from the everyday world
transformed by the respectful content of my vision.

Ira Ono
Whose Childhood, 2002
8 x 10 x 2 inches (20 x 25.5 x 5 cm)
Mixed media

Ira Ono
She Watches Us, 2003
16 x 24 x 2 inches (40 x 60 x 5 cm)
Mixed media

Fran Gardner Perry
Infinity, 2003
9½ x 6½ x 1 inches (24 x 16 x 2.5 cm)
Stitchery, maps, photos and found objects

Fran Gardner Perry

ARTIST STATEMENT: Through my work, I wish to honor the very specific and unique locations in the world that I have visited and found meaningful and sacred. Among these places are both the humble and fantastic—a rock in a stream or a rock face in a New Mexico canyon, a bleached maritime forest on the South Carolina coast, or the ocean floor at low tide in the Bay of Fundy. These bits of places, fragments of memories from my travels or my home, are translated into stitchery, combined with maps, photos, and found objects, and assembled into a product that is at once art and shrine. When I began to make these objects, I was sure they were too personal to my own experience, they wouldn't be understood without explanation. What I have found, however, is the human capacity to comprehend without specific knowledge of my intent. And what people understand

about my work, even without the explanation that I was so sure was necessary, is that the combination of objects and images reveals not specific meaning but a spiritual awareness. Viewers understand the symbolism of altars and the passage through the specific to the universal. As I have developed these pieces more and more towards the concept of shrines, I have often questioned my own compositional urges: Why do I need to combine a map of Mt. Ranier with a mural from the burnt ruins of Pompeii? But the work requires no outside approval and indeed, wouldn't be a shrine if outside approval were either sought or necessary. The shrine is brought about by the personal, by the very act of surrendering, placing the random gifts of imagery and objects together. And by the shrine's very existence, it speaks of reverence for this place where we live.

Fran Gardner Perry
Elevation 14,410, 2002
9½ x 6½ x 2½ inches
(24 x 16 x 5.5 cm)
Stitchery, maps, photos
and found objects

Fran Gardner Perry
Tidal Floes At Pritchard"s Island, 2002
9½ x 6½ x 1 inches
(16 x 24 x 2.5 cm)
Stitchery, maps, photos
and found objects

Nicole Tuggle

ARTIST STATEMENT: I am a mixed-media artist whose recent work has focused on collage and assemblage constructions. The beauty and mystery inherent in old, forgotten objects offer the opportunity to transform the ordinary into something sacred. Rusty metal hardware, worn wood, and paper scraps are rich raw materials waiting to be transformed into works of art. Creative alchemy is a worthwhile lesson in observation, seeing the potential in the everyday.

Nicole Tuggle
Blush, 2002
18⅛ x 17½ x 3 inches (46 x 45 x 7.5 cm)
Cash register drawer, vintage photos, medical illustrations, German sheet music, beeswax, cotton gauze, machine part, silver milagro

Nicole Tuggle
Flutter, 2003
6⅝ x 18 x 4½ inches (17 x 45 x 12 cm)
Wooden drawer, anatomical illustrations, entymology illustrations, paper, found writing, beeswax, clock parts, rusty scrap metal, mica

Graceann Warn

ARTIST STATEMENT: For 15 years assemblage has been my signature work, and I am still fascinated by it. I am using foundry patterns, old drawers, and antique boxes to house these worlds whose themes include celestial mechanics, Galileo, the natural sciences, travel, magic, and chance. These pieces continue to be pure fun to make, partly because of the collecting of the objects and partly because of the challenge of saying "just enough" and leaving the rest to the imagination. My goal with this work is for the viewer to enter and become involved in the story of the piece so that it becomes personal.

Graceann Warn
Great Big Sky Box, 2002
30 x 16 x 3 inches
(76 x 40 x 7.5 cm)
Oil on canvas, found
objects, carved theater
foam wings, wire
in vintage boxes

Graceann Warn
Icarus Box, 2003
16 x 7 x 5 inches (40 x 18 x 13 cm)
Paper, beeswax, glass, feather in vintage file drawer

Lynn Whipple

Lynn Whipple
Bobby, 2000
12 x 12 x 2 inches (30 x 30 x 5 cm)
Acrylic, collage, found objects

ARTIST STATEMENT: I have always been fascinated by old books, history, and odd bits memorabilia. I find the things that interest me most are slightly absurd. I am espec: fond of old photographs. These are the things that find their way into my work. In early stages of a piece I will begin with a collage, building a story and a surface. Sir pencil drawing is an important part of my work, as well as the written word—frag-ments from my thoughts, pages from old journals, forgotten letters. I don't wish the written word to become too obvious or contrived, so I usually obscure the surface, covering the words with paint or beeswax. My hope is to create something real and somehow poetic, yet not commonplace. My goal is to continue communicating in r own language. I feel very fortunate to be able to go through life doing something I love, and hopefully share it with others.

Lynn Whipple
Kind, 2001
6 x 8 x 2 inches (15 x 20 x 5 cm)
Collage, acrylic, pencil, muslin, found objects

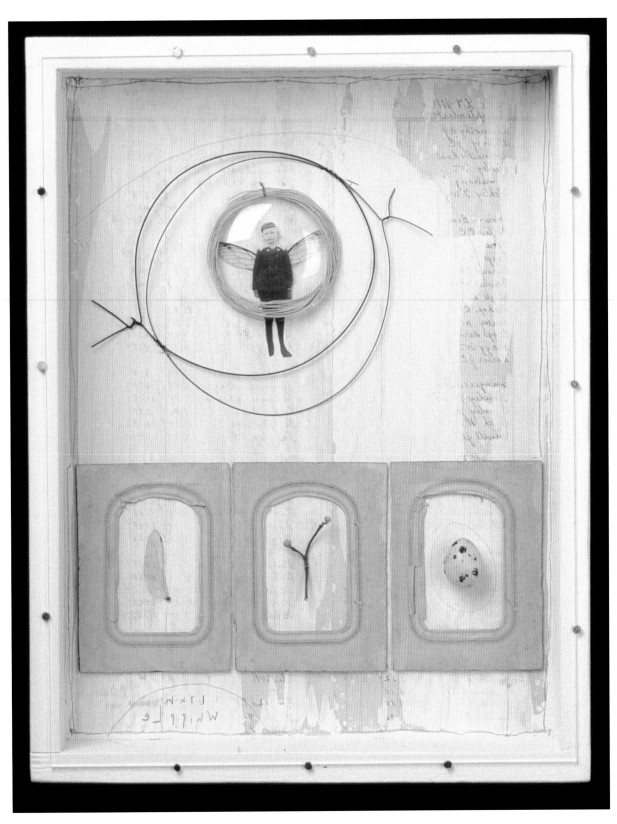

Lynn Whipple
Fly Boy, 2001
13 x 18 x 2 inches (33 x 46 x 5 cm)
Collage, acrylic, pencil, found objects

Joanne Williams

ARTIST STATEMENT: My collages are often inspired by found objects. I create stories and ceremonies from "cultural memories" which remain mysterious to me. In my work, I continue to explore the notion of art as contemplative space for viewers' participation and meditation. The process is a spiritual one for me—one of trust and balance in controlling the media and in letting go of it. Starting the process for my work involves "gathering"— bringing an idea to visualization so that I can begin to find the elements I will assemble to create the piece. Often I am not aware that I am searching for an element until I find myself discovering something—an item on the sidewalk, a stick on the beach, a fragment of jewelry—and I am drawn to it and take it to the studio. I understand the term "found" objects: they find me. This way of looking is about the endless search, and it results in abundant collections.

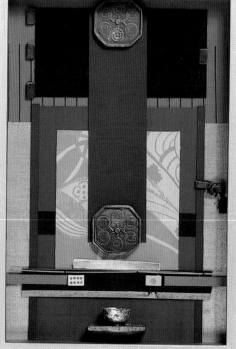

Joanne Williams
To the Sun, 2003
16½ x 46½ x 3 inches (21 x 116 x 7.5 cm)
Acrylic painting with encaustic and gold leaf, antique kimono silk, wood, found metal, bone mah-jongg tiles, Chinese coin replicas, Indian makeup box fragment, kimono tie

Joanne Williams
Flight, 2003 from *Carnivale* series
20 x 28 x 3 inches (51 x 71 x 7.5 cm)
Encaustic, acrylic gold leaf painting, wood, silk,
K'chinn weaving from Thailand.

Joanne Williams
Moon Bathing, 2002
12 x 60 x 3 inches
(30 x 153 x 7.5 cm)
Acrylic painting, silver
and gold leaf, wood,
antique kimono silk,
antique Chinese soap-
stone, chopstick holders,
sumi brush, kimono
tie, antique silver
Chinese box

Artist Biographies

Akira Blount was born in 1945 and has been interested in art all her life. Although she holds a degree in art education from the University of Wisconsin in Madison, she is essentially a self-taught doll maker. She learned needlework from her grandmother and got her interest in dolls from her mother. Akira has pursued her work with the doll form for more than 30 years. She is a full-time studio artist and teacher. She began as a fiber artist, but her recent work is mixed media. For the last several years, she has been collaborating with her husband Larry, a woodworker. Akira's work has been admired for many years by doll and fine craft aficionados and is included in private and museum collections around the world. Her work can be seen at akirastudios.com.

Beth Cote is a professional artist who works with mixed media and book arts, primarily focusing on altered books. She has taught art to both children and adults more than 10 years across the United States. As an art advocate, she spearheaded a volunteer group that taught art education at local elementary schools and wrote the art curriculum that resulted in the school board instituting an art program. She is the author of several books on altered books and has also produced videos on the subject. Her work has appeared in magazines including *Somerset Studio, Expressions,* and *Art Business News.* She is the founder and co-president of the International Society of Altered Book Artists. Her work can be seen at alteredbook.com.

Heidi Darr-Hope has been a professional artist for more than 20 years. Her work has been exhibited worldwide in galleries and museums and is included in many private and corporate collections including the South Carolina State Art Collection, Columbia Museum of Art, South Carolina State Museum, and the collections of Home Box Office, The Coca-Cola Company, and Marriott International. She has taught art to a diverse population ranging from senior citizens to at-risk teenagers to prisoners and students of all ages. Her work with individuals who are living with a life-threatening disease has broadened her approach to the arts. She sees art as a tool to enhance personal growth and development. Her work in the field of art and healing has extended from oncology to dealing with issues of bereavement, HIV/AIDS, and general therapeutics. You can see Heidi's work at darr-hope.com.

Nancy Hoerner was a freelance designer of cross-stitch embroidery for 20 years. For the last eight years, she has designed one-of-a-kind art dolls, many finding their way into magazines, shows, and galleries. Her love of paper art led to combining dolls and paper in a variety of forms. Most recently she has been combining collage and assemblage to create habitats, a collection of wooden boxes collaged and covered with architectural finds. She has been a member of the Society of Craft Designers for 16 years. Nancy teaches bookmaking in Jordan, Minnesota.

Janet Hofacker is a nationally known professional designer, artist, and writer. Her love of cloth and sewing as a girl led to the first of many creative endeavors that she has pursued over the years. She is an accomplished assemblage, collage, book art, and textile artist. Her original design projects and feature articles have appeared in numerous national magazines as well as in several books. Her artwork is in private collections and galleries throughout the United States, and Canada. She lives in Idaho.

Judy Hubbard is southern by birth and location, with roots that reach deep. In her South Carolina studio, a reclaimed barn that sits deep in the garden of her home, she stores a gatherer's treasure of found objects: broken clocks and watches, disassembled doll parts, buttons, feathers, old letters, photos. These unlikely treasures are sorted and stored in a library card catalogue made obsolete by the computer. Hubbard's mixed media constructions draw not only on these found materials, but also on her background in textile design. Judy can be contacted at jkhubbard@aol.com.

Inga Hunter is African-Australian. She was born in England and now lives in Australia. She has a BA in anthropology from the University of Sydney. She is an artist, tutor, writer, lecturer, and photographer. She has exhibited extensively throughout Australia. She can be contacted at ingagirvanhunter@bigpond.com.

Janice Lowry has been exhibiting her work for more than 30 years. She received a BFA and MFA from the Phoenix College Art Center of Design, and has taught there as well as at other places, including the Art Institute of California Orange County. She has led various journal workshops, as well. Her work has been in numerous exhibitions and featured in publications such as *Somerset Studio, Los Angeles Times,* and *Art Forum.* She is married and has three children and a dog, and lives in an old house near her studio in Santa Ana, California. Her work can be seen at Janicelowry.com.

Keith Lo Bue received a BFA in illustration and photography from Purchase College, State University of New York. He feels his real art education came from studying the paintings and sculpture at the Museum of Modern Art where he worked summers as a security guard while getting his degree. He began making jewelry and was much influenced by the box assemblages of Joseph Cornell. Born in Fairfax, Virginia, he now lives in Sydney, Australia, with his daughter Mira. He has been featured in numerous publications, and teaches workshops throughout Australia and the United States. His work can be seen at lobue-art.com.

Melissa Manley-Daniels holds a BA in art from the University of North Carolina at Wilmington. She lives in Wilmington and is currently pursuing her MFA in the metal design program at East Carolina University. She enjoys making found-object jewelry and creating mixed-media collage—from wall pieces to tiny assemblages—as well as altered books. When she is not creating art or being a mom or a student, she is gardening, working on her website or just curling up with a good book. Her work can be seen at manley-daniels.com.

Sharon McCartney grew up in a wooded area of western Pennsylvania and now lives and works in Lexington, Massachusetts. In addition to producing one-of-a-kind artist's books, she paints on wood and canvas, employing a collage approach and a vast range of media. Sharon can be contacted at lilypeek@aol.com.

Karen Michel is a mixed-media book artist, painter, and art journaler. She lives on Long Island, New York, where, with her husband Carlo Thertus, she runs a non-profit art center for kids and adults called the Creative Art Space for Kids Foundation. She attended the School of Visual Arts in New York City and the Institute of American Indian Arts in Santa Fe, New Mexico, studying fine arts. Her books, paintings, and collages have been exhibited interna-

and she can also be found teaching workshops around the United States. Her work can be seen at karen-michel.com.

Maria Consuelo Moya was born in Santa Fe, New Mexico, in 1947. She has studied in New Mexico, Israel, Norway, and Turkey. Her work is in collections throughout the United States and several foreign countries. She is a professional artist, teacher, lecturer, and exhibitor in galleries and invitational exhibits. Currently she works in her studio, Studio MCM, in Albuquerque, New Mexico. She can be contacted at studiomcm@earthlink.net.

Karron Nottingham was born in Little Falls, Minnesota, in 1959. She attended various art schools throughout her childhood, graduating from the University of Wisconsin, River Falls, in 1981. For several years she lived and worked on the island of Hawaii. Her work has been exhibited nationally and internationally, and she is a sought-after lecturer in women's studies on the subject of "Stories to Tell." She returned to Minnesota in 1997 and operates a studio in Minneapolis, teaching art enrichment classes to children. Her personal studio is located in her home in Marine on St. Croix, Minnesota. Her work appeared in the book *Paper Making in Basketry*, and in *Honolulu Magazine*. She does extensive corporate commission work, most recently for the Johnson Foundation, in Racine, Wisconsin. She can be contacted at knotti2401@aol.

Walter Nottingham received his MFA from Cranbrook Academy of Art and taught at the University of Wisconsin, River Falls, for 30 years, retiring as a professor emeritus of fine arts. He now resides and has his studio in Hilo, Hawaii. He has been a visiting artist and workshop instructor at various institutions throughout the United States, Canada, Australia, and New Zealand. His artworks have been exhibited and collected internationally, and he has received numerous awards, including the NEA Artist Grant. In 1988 he was elected into the American Crafts Council College of Fellows. In 2002 he recorded his oral history for the *Archives of American Art* in the Smithsonian Institution, Washington, DC. He can be reached at waltlee.gte.net.

Linda O'Brien and **Opie O'Brien** are married to one another and work individually and also collaboratively. Originally from New York City, they live in Ohio by Lake Erie where they share their house and recording studio with their cats Angelus and Angel. Opie is a mixed-media artist as well as a musician. He is a composer, arranger, and instrumentalist, and has played with major bands and music legends. Linda is a mixed-media artist, a writer, and a jewelry and stamp designer. Together they own Burnt Offerings Studio and have their own line of unmounted rubber art stamps for the mixed-media artist. They teach workshops nationally, using organic, recycled, and found materials. They appreciate the unusual, and collect everything from space toys to burial dolls. These themes influence their work, which has been featured in galleries, museums, magazines, books, CDs, on TV and in private collections. Their work can be seen at burntofferings.com.

Gena Ollendieck grew up in northeast Iowa, exploring the woods and prairies. A graduate of Central College in Pella, Iowa, with a degree in art and education, she was a Peace Corps volunteer in Paraguay, South America. She has studied bookbinding, paper decoration, and contemporary book arts for more than 10 years. She is a full-time artist in northeast Iowa, and teaches book arts at local colleges, private schools, and workshops around the Midwest. She can be contacted at indigostar40@hotmail.com.

Ira Ono is a multifaceted visual and performing artist well-known in Hawaii for his innovative work. He is an artist who engages the viewer with a wide range of media and subject matter. Much of his inspiration comes from living in a rain forest in Hawaii. He can be contacted at iraono@Hawaii.rr.com.

Lynne Perrella is an illustrator, mixed-media artist, and writer. She is the owner of Acey Duecy Rubber Stamps and makes regular contributions to various paper-arts publications and books. Her main art interest is in forms of layering, including collage and assemblage, one-of-a-kind books, and journals. Her interest in teaching comes from an enjoyment of sharing the creative sandbox with other kindred artists and making mutual discoveries in a supportive and enthusiastic environment. She is the author of *Artists' Journals and Sketchbooks: Exploring and Creating Personal Pages*. Her work can be seen at LKPerrella.com.

Fran Gardner Perry took her first textile course in college in 1982, and since then she has been working in the medium of fabric and stitchery. In 1993, she completed her MFA studies at Vermont College of Norwich University. There she studied with such notable artists as Napoleon Jones-Henderson, Lee Malerich, Heidi Darr-Hope, and art historian/author Janet Kaplan. Perry's stitchery work has found many venues, most notably *Fiberarts Design Book V*, published by Lark Books in 1995. In addition, her works have been displayed in solo and group exhibits, winning awards in many juried competitions. Perry lives in Lancaster, South Carolina, where she teaches studio art and art history at the University of South Carolina Lancaster. She is also the curator of Hubbard Hall Gallery at

the university. You can contact her at fperry@gwm.sc.edu.

Madonna Phillips is a member of the Piedmont Craftsman's Guild and the Carolina Designer Craftsmen's Guild. She lives in the historic Oakwood neighborhood of downtown Raleigh, North Carolina, with her husband, Greg Hallam, a city planner. She maintains a studio at Artspace in Raleigh's City Market. She has exhibited her work extensively throughout the United States. She can be contacted at design58@aol.com.

Gayle Pritchard is a well-known fiber artist whose career has spanned some 20 years. In addition, she is a curator, lecturer, teacher, and published writer. Gayle studied art at the College of Wooster, Paul Valery University in France, the Surface Design Symposium in Columbus, Ohio, and the Cleveland Institute of Art. Her work has been widely exhibited in galleries and museums across the United States and in Denmark, Japan, and Australia. Highlight exhibitions include the Cleveland Museum of Art, Ohio Designer Craftsmen Best of '94, and Visions, an international fiber exhibition in San Diego. Commissions include the Rock and Roll Hall of Fame Quilt, the Smithsonian Craft Archives, and the Peter Lewis Building in Cleveland, Ohio. She is featured in the 1997 Encyclopedia of Living Artists, and was named Teacher of

the Year by *Professional Quilter Magazine*. She can be contacted at GAPDesigns@comcast.net.

Judi Riesch is a mixed-media artist living in Philadelphia with John, her husband of 34 years. They have two children, Jennifer and Christian. Judi has a BA in art education and an MA in media arts. Her work has been shown in galleries in Pennsylvania and the Southwest, and has been featured in many magazines including *Somerset Studio*, *Rubberstampmadness*, the *Studio Zine*, and *Play: The Art of Visual Journals*. Her work has also appeared in many books including *Collage for the Soul: Expressing Your Hopes and Dreams Through Art*; *Altered Books, Collaborative Journals, Other Adventures in Bookmaking*; *Artist's Journals and Sketchbooks, Exploring and Creating Personal Pages*; and *True Colors: A Palette of Collaborative Art Journals*. You can see her work at itsmysite.com/judiriesch.

Dorrit Title is a graduate of the Cooper Union School of Art and has a BFA from the San Francisco Art Institute. Her work has been exhibited at the Nassau County Museum of Art, the Islip Art Museum, the Heckscher Museum of Art, at Queensborough Community College (where her work is in the permanent collection), and many other locations. Her work is included in the anthology, *Bittersweet Legacy: Creative Responses to the Holocaust,* University Press of America. Her solo exhibits include the Rockland Center for Holocaust Studies and The Holocaust Memorial and Educational Center of Nassau County in Glen Cove, New York. She can be contacted at doho@optonline.net.

Nicole Tuggle has a lengthy background in paper crafts, collage, and mail art. Her artistic path has been as much about chronicling her own life as it has been about communicating and stimulating an emotional response from the viewer. She recently stumbled upon found-object assemblage out of a desire to further explore three-dimensional work. Nicole lives in Asheville, North Carolina, in a renovated old bank building with her digital-media-artist boyfriend. You can see her work at sigilation.com.

Luann Udell of Keene, New Hampshire, is an award-winning nationally exhibited mixed-media artist and jewelry maker. She is a double-juried member of the League of New Hampshire Craftsmen for stitchery and nonmetal jewelry. She authored *Rubber Stamp Carving*, published by Lark Books in 2002. Luann attended the University of Michigan, receiving a BA in art history and an MA in education. Her studio, Durable Goods, established in 1995, is now located in a restored antique post-and-beam barn at her home in Keene. You can see her work at durable-goods.com.

Graceann Warn received a Bachelor of Landscape Architecture from Michigan State University. She studied theater design and classical art and archeology, and did landscape architecture graduate work at the University of Michigan. She has exhibited her work across the United States at numerous galleries and craft shows, such as the Philadelphia Museum of Art Craft Show and the Smithsonian Craft Show, and has done both corporate and private commissions. Her work has appeared in many publications, including *Dance, American Craft*, *American Style*, and *FIBERARTS*. She has been a workshop instructor at Haystack Mountain School of Crafts, Hollander's School of Book and Paper Arts, University of Michigan Comprehensive Cancer Center's art therapy program, and the Ann Arbor Art Center. Her work can be seen at graceannwarn.com.

Lynn Whipple was born and raised in Winter Park, Florida, and shares a warehouse studio with her husband, John, who is also an artist. They live on a lake and are constantly inspired by the beauty of the wildlife. She is mostly self-taught, but credits her favorite teacher, David Passalaqua of Parson's School of Design, for showing her how to learn and see and always be true to her own voice. Her work has been shown nationally in galleries, museums, and juried shows, and has received numerous awards. She has been featured in many publications including *Creative Collage for Crafters*, *Mary Engelbreit's Home Companion,* and *New American Paintings*. Her work can be seen at whippleart.com.

Joanne Williams received an MFA in painting from George Washington University, and Corcoran College of Art and Design, in Washington, DC. She has won many awards for her painting. Sixteen years ago she began working in mixed media. Her work is in the collection of the Museum of Contemporary Arts and Design, New York City, and in many corporate and private collections. She has exhibited in the United States and London, and her work is in many galleries in the United States. She can be contacted at sacred47@aol.com.

Bibliography

The Atlas of Mysterious Places: The World's Unexplained Symbolic Sites, Ancient Cities and Lost Lands; Jennifer Westwood, editor; Barnes & Noble Books, 1997.

Beautiful Necessity: The Art and Meaning of Women's Altars; Kay Turner; Thames & Hudson, 1999.

Celebration: A World of Art and Ritual, Smithsonian Institution Press, 1982.

The Encyclopedia of the Ancient World; Charlotte Hurdman, Philip Steele, and Richard Tames; Anness Publishing Ltd., 2000.

The Language of the Goddess; Marija Gimbutas, Thames & Hudson, 2001.

Living Shrines: Home Altars of New Mexico; Marie Romero Cash; Museum of New Mexico Press, 1998.

Mythology: The Illustrated Anthology of World Myth and Storytelling; C. Scott Littleton, editor; Thunder Bay Press, 2002.

Sacred Imagery; Judith Millidge; World Publications, Inc., 1998.

Index

Acknowledgments

This book has been a joy to do because of the wonderful staff at Lark. Deborah Morgenthal came to me with the idea, and wouldn't take no for an answer. Many thanks to Ronni Lundy, my editor, for her generous help. She held my hand through the process, and became a friend. Susan McBride, the art director, and photographers Keith and Wendy Wright used their skills to make everything look good.

My artist friend, Delores Hamilton, was brave enough to test my how-to directions and gave me very helpful feedback. Walter Nottingham, a gifted teacher and my mentor for many years, helped guide my work to become what it is today.

And a special thanks to the guest artists who so generously allowed me to use their work and their words, and helped enrich the book you're holding in your hands.